Harvey

To me show-jumping has always been far
more than winning money. I suppose the great
majority of sportsmen, especially in sports
where it is one man against the rest, see their
part in it as a challenge.

There has never been anything I like better
than to buy a horse, improve it and then go
on to beat all the others. This is particularly
true in the case of a misfit with whom other
riders have been unable to get on. Among
my later horses, Salvador falls into that
category; War Paint was one of my early
ones. . . .

Harvey Smith

Harvey

Harvey Smith
with Victor Green

Arrow Books

Arrow Books Limited
3 Fitzroy Square, London W1

An imprint of the Hutchinson Publishing Group

London Melbourne Sydney Auckland
Wellington Johannesburg and agencies
throughout the world

First published Arrow Books 1976
© Harvey Smith and Victor Green 1976

Made and printed in Great Britain
by The Anchor Press Ltd
Tiptree, Essex

ISBN 0 09 913000 3

Parts of this book originally appeared in Harvey Smith's
Harvesting Success published by Pelham Books in 1968.

Contents

ACKNOWLEDGEMENTS

Photographs in order of appearance: Bingley Guardian, Irish Times, Daily Express (Brian Puff), Peter Sweetman, BBC, Manchester Daily Mail, Don Morley, Manchester Daily Mail, Don Morley.

Cartoons: Keith Waite (Daily Mirror), Rigby (The Sun), Giles (The Daily Express).

Introduction

My clashes with show-jumping's establishment have been news for as long as I've been in the sport. Dorian Williams summed up the thinking of the establishment when he once wrote in a book about show-jumping personalities: 'It may be that Harvey Smith is too ruthless, that he has got his values wrong, that he attaches too much importance to winning and too little to the sheer enjoyment of the sport.'

Later, in the same piece, he wrote: 'There are people – riders as well as legislators and organizers – who consider his influence in show-jumping undesirable, even subversive: that his insistence on a rigorously professional approach to the sport has taken the fun out of it, has made it all too serious and commercial.' Controversy had always surrounded me, he said, because I was a natural leader and had come to be regarded as the leader of the 'new set, the new approach'.

It has always been assumed by the press and the establishment that I go looking for trouble. I hope this book will set the record straight. I believe in the enjoyment to be gained from show-jumping as much as anyone – I like to think that I have helped to make the sport more widely popular over the last few years than it has ever been.

But our sport is only worth watching when it's truly competitive and the old-fashioned 'Come on, boys, let's have a jolly good time' attitude is now strictly for the hunting field.

Ever since I won my first major competition at Barnsley over twenty years ago my aim has always been to do my best to win.

If that's the 'new approach', I'm for it all the way.

Harvey Smith

1. Warming up

My family's one and only link with horses in past generations is represented by my mother's grandfather, who used to have the lifeboat horses at Bridlington. He was a hunting farmer with land near the beach and his working horses were always at the ready in case of an emergency which called for the lifeboat. It was a risky job and Mother told me once of the wild night when the boat turned over and the entire team of horses was swept out to sea and drowned. Their bodies were washed up on the beach next day.

So far as my life with horses is concerned, I have always been my own boss, mainly because horsy connections in the family are in the distant past and, apart from my introduction to ponies, the interest has had to come from me. Neither of my parents was interested in riding and it was my brother John, who is seven years older than I am, who first put me up on a pony – when I was seven. He borrowed a Shetland from someone he knew and later bought it after it had broken loose in its owner's garden and smashed all his cold frames.

John used to lead me about on it and I was not keen on the idea at all. What little enthusiasm I had disappeared altogether one day when the Shetland shied at one of John's goats and put me on the floor.

'That's it,' I told John. 'I'm not going to ride any more.' However, he persevered, kidding me on, and when he bought a horse for himself we began riding out together for longer distances. One regular ride was over Gilstead moors to see the late Laurie Glover, who had stables there, and later I began to ride a pony or two for Laurie.

I got a bit of showing experience and then was asked

by Jack Baker, a Bingley farmer, if I would ride for him. He had a few ponies for his milk round and it was on one of these, Simon, that I had my first experience of competition jumping, at Bingley Show. The year was 1947 and I was eight. Simon was new to the game like me, but we didn't do badly and later we struck up a good partnership in gymkhanas. Because the ponies had to work every morning pulling the carts and we had to travel far afield for competitions, I got to only a handful of shows in the next three years. And at those I did get to it was gymkhana work more than show-jumping that I went in for. Simon went on working long after I outgrew him and was still in good health when killed by lightning in 1963.

At the time that I was riding for Jack Baker, and helping to feed and generally look after his ponies, I did a school-boy swap which as it turned out was to have a pronounced effect on my life. A pair of bicycle handlebars I had proved to be worth a sheepdog puppy in the eyes of a friend of mine from a local farm and I soon found out that this pup was very quick at learning tricks. In fact, they seemed to come naturally to her. I taught her to carry eggs, to jump through a hoop, then to jump through a hoop carrying a hoop in her mouth, and when I invited someone to put a handkerchief down among a dozen others the dog was able to pick out the right handkerchief and return it to its owner.

She built up a good enough repertoire for me to enter her for competitions, and I suppose it was through her that I first realized that I enjoyed entertaining people. At one local talent competition there was a girl saxophonist among the rival contestants, and it was through her that I came to know Lionel Whittingham who, years later, helped me buy a horse called Farmer's Boy. My black and white dog, by the way, won second prize and invitations followed for me to give demonstrations at sheepdog trials and so on. After a while I teamed up with Cyril Belshaw, who used to train a group of Alsatians, and I got a great deal of enjoyment from our outings.

I began to see more of Lionel, as at that time he was

beginning to get interested in ponies and we both used to go to Botterill's Sales at York. He took the plunge into ownership in 1952 by buying a two-year-old filly by a thoroughbred stallion out of a pony mare who was very near 'clean-bred' herself. We had fiddled about with Lady Opal, as she was called, for a while when one day I said to Lionel that it was time we broke her in properly. A few minutes later he went home for a cup of tea and when he came back I was riding her across the fields. All I had done was laid myself across her back, cocked my leg over and then allowed her to stand until she wanted to move forward. I had 'mouthed' her earlier with a key bit and within five weeks of first getting up on her she was in the ring under saddle.

Lady Opal was a good-looking filly and she won a good few classes against ponies much her senior. On one occasion, when a number of top-class ponies made the trip over to Bingley after the Royal Lancashire Show, she beat all but one of them. She was the second pony I had broken in, the first being one bred by my brother out of the Shetland on which I had learned to ride, and by a Welsh Mountain stallion. We called him Amby, after Amby Ainsworth, a gypsy dealer I used to cycle over the moors to talk horses with as a very young lad. Amby turned out to be a clever little jumper, only 11.2 hands high but capable of clearing five feet for the fun of it.

The year before I left school I went to Todmorden, the town that is part Yorkshire and part Lancashire, to show Lady Opal and ride another pony in the gymkhana. Todmorden Show was a fairly big affair but what I saw in the jumping classes did not impress me. 'If we can't get a horse to do that then it's a rum job,' I told my companion, Lionel Whittingham.

I was fifteen at the time and I had done only a bit of junior jumping. Yet it seemed to me that we should not have much difficulty in finding a horse capable of beating what I had seen that afternoon.

The fact that we were as green as grass didn't stop us

from hurrying off to the next Botterill's Sale down by the Ouse at York and buying a six-year-old mare, Rose Marie. So far as we knew, she had never jumped a fence in her life although she had been backed. I taught her what bit I knew about jumping and was quite satisfied when she began to pick up prize money in novice classes.

Around this time I started to take more interest in jumping, and my visit to Todmorden with Lady Opal left me in no doubt that it would be worth while to have a go. The week after Lionel and I bought Rose Marie I went on holiday with my parents to Petersfield where, realizing that I was serious about jumping, my father took me into a bookshop and bought me the one book I have ever read on the sport – Count Toptani's *Modern Show-Jumping,* subtitled 'The South American Method'. I read snatches of the book during a week in which I was fretting to get back to Rose Marie, for I really was getting double keen on the job.

I schooled her at home and she won enough small prizes to make me satisfied with her and my progress. I stayed satisfied until I managed to buy a big bay four-year-old out of a draught mare just over on the boat from Ireland.

2. Farmer's Boy

The horse was Farmer's Boy and he, more than any other horse, really got me going in show-jumping. I came across him in March 1954 at Botterill's Sale. What I liked about him when Lionel Whittingham and I saw him being jogged up and down the passage-way in that cramped and soon-to-be-scrapped sale area was that he was a cocksure fellow. I was sick to have him and watched closely as he was knocked down for thirty-three guineas. I hadn't any cash with me so I dashed to a phone box outside and rang my father. Hardly hesitating, he replied: 'Borrow the money from Lionel and buy him.'

When I got back in the sale premises and sought out the buyer, I found he had already passed the horse on at a small profit. After a search, I was taken to the new owner and he was happy to take a small profit himself. The amount I had to pay was just £40.

In those days the railways still had plenty of wagons for horses and Botterill's arranged the transport from York to my home town of Bingley in the West Riding. The horse was brought from the station and popped into the loose box next to Rose Marie's just behind the yard of my father's building contractor's business at Gilstead. Partly because he showed a bit of feather on his heels, I gave him the name Farmer's Boy. The day after his arrival at Gilstead, I put a bridle on him – using a jointed snaffle – got up on him and with Paul Swindon, a friend of mine, giving us a lead on Rose Marie, Farmer's Boy and I set off across the moors on our first outing. I don't think he had been backed or mouthed in Ireland.

Within a month he was at his first show. When I started

schooling him at home I put him first of all at a fence three feet or so high and from that point raised the height steadily until he was clearing five feet without any trouble. A very slow style of jumping came naturally to him and I fell in with this. Not that he was a sluggard, for he was very agile and turned out to be capable of holding his own with the best in the country against the clock.

At his first appearance in public, at East Hardwick, near Pontefract, I entered him in both the Grade C and the Open and he had only one fence down in each of them. Three shows later he took second place in the Grade C at Nelson, in Lancashire, and next time out he got his first red rosette when he divided with the famous Flanagan in a big Open at Barnsley. Jim Cowen was riding Flanagan for Mr Robert Hanson (Pat Smythe took him over later) and there was a good field behind us for in those days such horses as Valencia, Huntsman, Hack On, Leicester Lad and Prudence were competing regularly in the north.

The year 1954, the one in which I bought Farmer's Boy, I left school and started working for the family building firm. In my early show-jumping days the reporters persisted in calling me a former bricklayer, but, more accurately, they should have called me a former bulldozer driver or former plumber, for I spent longer plumbing and driving diggers and bulldozers than I did mastering the art of laying bricks.

Initially, I was only a weekend jumper, for my father died the year after I joined the building firm and my time was pretty well filled in the building trade. Gradually, I took more of an executive position with the firm until at the age of twenty-five I became a partner in it with my elder brother, John. For a while I helped with the administrative work and then I broke with both the building company and another one we had formed. I was too involved with show-jumping and my farm to give useful service to them.

To return to my first season with Farmer's Boy in 1954. Despite our only competing at weekends, Farmer's Boy was in the money sixteen times and he showed his potential by getting placed in a strong Open class at Southport after his tie with Flanagan. His progress continued in his record season when I made my first trip south, to Taunton, and later he won a hot novice class at Blackburn, the Dorothy Pawson Grade C Championship, from Seamus Hayes and Pucka Poona.

To end the 1955 season I took Farmer's Boy down to Harringay for our first look at an indoor show. He did not care a lot for it, but quickly settled in and gave of his best, as he did throughout his life. All told, Farmer's Boy won or was placed twenty-five times in 1955, four more than in 1956 when I had to spend more time with the family firm. Farmer's Boy, however, did show his best-ever form in winning the Southport Championship beating such good ones as Costa, Pegasus, Nugget and Dusty Miller.

I was still feeling my way in the game, but, having sold Rose Marie, I bought an interestingly bred horse from Sir Benjamin Dawson at York. Sir Benjamin kept a few Suffolk Punch mares and bred them to Porter's Call, a very good miler in his day. Leonard Jowett had one of the offspring in Bingley which I liked the look of, so I went over to Sir Benjamin's place and bought one, a three-year-old. I called him Andrew and produced him the next year. He was chosen for the Olympic squad in 1959 but, while there was no fence he could not clear he would always have a fence or two down – a 'four-faulter', in other words.

Andrew came third on his début at Otley and less than a month later he gained his first win in a good novice class at Todmorden. Generally, though, 1957 was a quiet year and Farmer's Boy wasn't out until July. He ended his short season at the Horse of the Year Show. In the *Daily Telegraph* contest he was the only horse in the two sections to jump a clear and there were more than forty forward in each section. I remember it was a combination of a parallel into a triple bar which caused all the trouble. It is said by some people that the faults should be evenly spread over the whole course, but if one fence is proving troublesome it is up to the riders to get the answer to it. After all, the fences are there to sort out the riders.

3. Breakthrough

So came 1958 – the year which marked, I suppose, my real arrival in show-jumping. Andrew had a light time and was turned out in the fields all summer. Occasionally I brought him out just for the afternoon, jumped him at a show and then popped him back in the fields at night. He was a good sort and managed this routine on what grazing he found for himself.

I travelled Mudlark, a horse I had bought for £60, with Farmer's Boy and for them the season began fairly early at Ascot. Both were placed, and Farmer's Boy continued to win minor prizes up to July when Lionel and I set off with him for the White City and to the turning-point in my show-jumping career.

The usual formidable international entry at the White City included a strong American team and two of the three riders on whom I had based my style – Raimondo d'Inzeo and Pat Smythe. I paid special attention to Raimondo rather than his brother, Piero, the more famous of the two at the time, because he had been on the worse horses of the two and yet had got a very good tune out of them. He kept his horses more together, too, whereas Piero let them move on, and it was the former style which more appealed to me. Pat Smythe's method was similar to Raimondo's. Her horses were always on an even rhythm, always balanced, and they could jump from any stride. That, I think, is why she had the tremendous success she did.

The third rider I watched closely in my early days was Dawn Palethorpe. She had been hitting the jackpot, too, with Earlsrath Rambler, although in 1958 she passed him back to her sister Jill.

During that White City week I tried not to miss watching a single round and at the same time I got down to analysing the courses in a more thorough way than I had done before. The fences themselves, with the exception of those put up in the later stages of the King George V Cup, were not daunting. Weekend competition in the north was so hot then that Farmer's Boy and I had become used to far bigger tracks than those built down country.

He went as well as I could have hoped all week, notching up the most important win to date for me in the Young Riders' International Championship from Ann Barker, sister of internationals William and David Boston, on Lucky Sam. Farmer's Boy went second in the jump-off and pipped Lucky Sam on time. My bay horse then made the southerners really sit up and take notice by reaching the last round of the King George V Cup – the only British horse to do so. He finished sixth behind the famous American rider, Hugh Wiley, on Master William, and later was seventh in the *Daily Mail* Cup.

The outcome of Farmer's Boy's good form was that, right out of the blue, Colonel Harry Llewellyn, then chief selector for the British Show Jumping Association, came up and asked me if I would go with the British team to Dublin as a replacement for an intended member who had lost his touch. I didn't possess a red jacket and after I arrived home, had less than one week to get one made. The tailor beat the deadline but my lack of an evening-dress suit was to be the cause of a bit of amusement.

After just a few days at home, Jill Banks (formerly Pale-thorpe) and her husband Stewart drove over from Nafferton in the East Riding, picked up Farmer's Boy and myself in their box and we all made our way to Holyhead for the boat trip to Dublin and my first show outside Britain.

I had heard a lot about Dublin Week and the liveliness of the Dublin Show crowd, but I never imagined the social side could be quite so wild or the arena so full of atmosphere. That week turned out to be one of the happiest times I have spent with a British team. It was, of course, my first trip and it has special memories because of that, but I don't think I have known members of a team quite so willing to help each other or to get on so well together.

George Hobbs, the captain, was a real 'mucker-in', Marshall Charlesworth is one of the nicest fellows anyone could wish to meet, and Jill Banks is the tops. We had some great fun at the dances and other social functions, though my movements were somewhat restricted. The restrictions were imposed by an evening suit kindly lent to me by Colin Leach, who used to groom for Donald Wright, another northern rider. The trouble was that Colin is only about five feet three inches and I am not far short of six feet. Jill found the solution by sewing me into the suit every night, fly and all. Jill also helped me in that her groom did both Rambler and Farmer's Boy, and he plaited up my horse for the very first time.

When I first rode into the main ring at Ballsbridge and saw the huge crowd – on Nations Cup Day it was almost 50 000 – I felt a twinge of nervousness as I had before the final jump-off in the King George. It went quickly and never again have I felt the slightest trace. We were rank outsiders for the Nations Cup and the press suggested that Britain had slighted the show by sending 'a bricklayer, a farmer's son [Marshall], a housewife and an ex-steeplechase jockey'. We were not upset by these criticisms because we knew our horses were all there on form and not on past reputations and when we had a get-together on the eve of the Nations Cup we vowed we could and would make the critics eat their words.

As soon as we saw the course we knew for certain that we were in with a good chance. It was a bit trappy, with short distances, and suited our horses down to the ground. Farmer's Boy, Rambler, Royal Lord and Smokey Bob all were old-type BSJA horses; that is, they would jump straight up-and-down fences all day long, while the Americans, our most dangerous rivals that day, gallop on more and do best when the distances are longer.

Colonel Nat Kindersley was the chef d'équipe and we

caused him a bit of worry before the competition began.
My bay horse needed just a couple of jumps before any big
class and usually I put up a straight pole at 5 feet 6 inches
or so. Anyway, I built one of these and went hurtling down
towards it, watched in the distance by Colonel Kindersley.

Farmer's Boy hit it, bang, right on his shins, and this
prompted the Colonel to come dashing towards me. What
he was about to say I will never know, for he was intercepted
by the late Wally Hobbs, brother of George, a man with
a gift for correcting riders' faults although he has never
ridden in his life. In colourful language he asked the Colonel
to retire to the stands and leave the schooling to us. It was as
well that the request was granted, for George promptly
turned his horse right over. The eventful preliminaries
concluded, we got down to the competition proper.

Smokey Bob was the first to go and after a refusal at the
third had only one time fault, to make his score four.
Rambler also had four, whereas both George Hobbs' Royal
Lord and my horse went clear. Ksar d'Esprit and Bill
Steinkraus were clear for the United States, but the rest of
the team did moderately and none of the Portuguese,
French or Irish horses had a clear. Barring a bad fall from
form, we had it all sewn up. The chef d'équipe was there to
make sure no unnecessary slip-up did occur and as Farmer's
Boy was bang on the time limit in the first round he asked
me to wake him up before I took him in again. Rumour
has it that I replied. 'T'old 'oss won't be bustled.' Anyway,
I had to refuse his request because if I ever tried to push
Farmer's Boy on he was just not the same horse.

Allowed to jump in his normal way, I could put him
exactly where I wanted him. If I threw a handkerchief anywhere within reason in front of a fence I could place his
front feet bang on that spot. It was too dangerous to change
our method then, so he went his own way and did very well
again, faulting only at the water, which also caught Rambler
and Smokey Bob. Royal Lord did even better, jumping
his second clear round and giving us an unbeatable total
overall of twelve faults. The Americans came with a rush,

adding only half a time fault to their first-round score, but it was too late to catch us. The fact that the Irish were fifth and last did not prevent the crowd giving us a terrific ovation.

Once back home, Farmer's Boy continued to catch his share of placings and finished fifth to Flanagan in the Olympic trial at the British Timken Show. Sadly, it was around this time that he began to have trouble with one of his forelegs. I tried everything – special shoes, more regular shoeing, keeping his foot in clay – but all to no avail, and eventually, in the spring of 1959, I took him down to a Cheshire veterinary surgeon. An X-ray confirmed that he had navicular, an incurable bone disease, and I left him to be unnerved in the affected leg. There were no satisfactory drugs in those days and I was told that the operation could give him up to eight more years in show-jumping. As Farmer's Boy was still only nine, I thought the operation was worth doing.

The operation was carried out on countless carthorses in the olden days to keep them working and is a simple one involving the opening of the skin and the parting of the nerve. Farmer's Boy was laid off for a month after the operation but as soon as he came into work again he showed lame in the other foreleg. Back to Cheshire he went for a repeat on that leg and again he had a month to recover. Because of all this, his début for the 1959 season was delayed until July. For a while I felt my way with him and then he suddenly hit top form. His winning run began with the Liverpool Championship and by the end of the season he had another twenty-three firsts to his credit, including the Leading Show Jumper title at Wembley, new home of the Horse of the Year Show.

While Farmer's Boy was having his legs attended to, I was invited to join the Olympic training squad for a fortnight's training course at Arundel in Sussex. It was a big squad, consisting of Jill Banks, Mary Barnes, Ann Townsend, Marshall Charlesworth, Peter Robeson, David Barker, Lieutenant-Colonel 'Monkey' Blacker, Douglas Bunn and

Captain the Hon. John Brooke. When the short-list was announced nine months later only two of the original squad were on it and finally only David Barker, with the inexperienced ex-racehorse Franco, made the team for Rome. We all stayed at a pub in Arundel and the horses were stabled at Goodwood. The days passed quickly as there were the horses to collect and bring back to Arundel before our work-outs with the late Colonel Jack Talbot-Ponsonby, trainer to the squad, and there were lectures on stable management, shoeing and so on.

Andrew never was true Olympic material, although he kept building up my hopes. He could jump absolutely anything and they were unable to build a fence down there which could beat him. Put one up 6 feet high by 6 feet wide and he would jump it clean nine times out of ten. Put up one 3 feet high by 3 feet wide and he would jump that nine times out of ten, too. As I said before he was a 'four-faulter'. Nevertheless, Andrew was a good horse on his day and in a so-called Olympic trial among all the horses at Arundel he finished second to Bandit, who was a brilliant jumper at that time.

I did not hit it off with Colonel Talbot-Ponsonby. He tried to get everyone to fit a pattern and it didn't work in my case. For instance he built a combination that Andrew could jump comfortably in two strides but could not cope with in one, and the trainer kept telling me that we must jump it in one. Well, if you can do something a lot easier one way than you can another I think you should do it the easy way. We just did not see eye to eye.

All in all, I was not sorry that I had been invited on the course, for nothing done with horses is a waste of time. I didn't jump Andrew after July by which time Farmer's Boy was sound again. Once his winning streak began he was pretty near invincible, and when I took him up to the Caledonian at Falkirk he finished up with four firsts, two seconds and a third to give me my first award for leading rider of the show.

Wembley began a fortnight later and Farmer's Boy won

four firsts there also, his outstanding win coming in the Leading Show Jumper of the Year competition in which we finished up jumping one of the biggest courses I have faced in my life. The fence that caused the trouble was a triple bar into a straight-up poles with a distance of ten yards between them. If they tried to come out in one stride the horses flattened on it and took the far bar and very few were clever enough to do it in two. My old fellow was, though, and only Bandit, Ann Townsend's good horse, survived with him for a third and last round. Farmer's Boy went clear again, jumping what I think was the best round of his career. Bandit could not stay with him and chalked up sixteen faults. I collected the rosette just before midnight, having begun in the qualifying round at just after eight o'clock in the morning.

At the end of the show I was awarded the Wembley Spurs for the most points in national competitions on one horse.

I had also picked up a bit on a recent addition to my stable, Montana. He had been a good horse with Ted Williams and had gone from him to 'Tucker' Makin when he came out of ponies after years of consistent winning. Montana took to refusing with Tucker in 1958, as he did later when Gillian Makin took him over. I got interested in him and at the Harewood three-day event in 1959 I asked George Thackray, a local farmer who was then part-owner, what he intended to do with the horse. 'If you want him, you can take him,' he replied. 'Go shoot him if you want to.' His feelings were understandable for Montana's winnings for the season up to then – September – stood at £23.

I picked him up the following Sunday convinced that all that was wrong with him was that he had lost confidence in his riders and, sure enough, when I climbed aboard him at home away he went. Six days later he was third in a good Open class at Keighley, shortly after that he shared first place with Farmer's Boy at the Nidderdale Show and at Wembley the next month he was equal first in the Overture and the *Daily Telegraph* Stakes. I had no difficulty with him at all, and although he was inclined to put in a very occasional stop, he did so only when he was feeling the hard ground.

In most cases all that is wrong with horses who pack it in, like Montana and like War Paint and Sea Hawk who joined me later, is that they have been forced into trouble by their jockeys and, as a result, have lost their confidence. It hurts them when their jockeys land them in the middle of a fence and their reaction is to think: 'Blow that for a lark.' It is always the best jumpers who chuck it in early, because they are the ones who are naturally careful and do not want to hit anything. Deliberate Dans who do not mind mowing them all down will never stop. My confidence seems to get across to these horses who have become unsure of themselves and have lost all confidence in their riders.

4. On the international circuit

There were occasions in those early days when I entered gymkhanas if I had failed to cover expenses in the jumping classes. Mudlark, in particular, was handy at the game and once – at Birkenshaw – when I had had a bad day he won all three Open gymkhana classes. At £3 a time that meant a useful £9, although it didn't please Miss Irene Shuttleworth, the girl who later became Mrs Smith. She used to take a dim view of my 'taking the youngsters' money' but they were Open classes, I reminded her, and I was entitled to enter.

Irene had not done any riding before I met her, but she quickly picked it up and regularly rode work for me in the three years I knew her before our marriage in May 1960. At the start of that season my stables were fuller than ever before, housing Farmer's Boy, Montana, Mudlark, Zena and Andrew. My one regular helper, Paul Swindon, had disappeared from the scene some time earlier when he set up in business on his own.

Realizing that neither Andrew nor Mudlark was going to reach the top in jumping, I sold them. Andrew went to Lincolnshire as a hunter and did very well. I knew that he was a real good horse across country before I sold him from his performance when I once rode him round the European three-day event course at Harewood. At that time I was thinking ahead and toying with the idea of eventing although show-jumping soon put those thoughts out of my head.

The two main strings to my bow were Farmer's Boy and Montana and with them I made the firm switch to the county circuit. They performed just as well as they had in the locals. The courses were bigger, especially the spreads, and the competition was hotter, but on the whole the horses did not have to get more height. Northern local shows have always been much harder to win than local shows in the south and the fences have a habit of getting quite high.

I got in three or four shows before the wedding. Irene and I had chosen to live in a caravan sited only a few hundred yards from my old home behind which were the stables. Irene's early married life was spent travelling all over the country as my groom and in sharing the job of looking after enough chickens to keep us busy when we were at home.

Farmer's Boy and Montana showed their appreciation by hitting great form, ending up seventh and around eleventh in the British Show Jumping Association Top Twenty, despite both being lamed at the Lincolnshire County Show in June and having to be laid off for a month.

Apart from the Lincoln incident, Farmer's Boy's legs held up well and he enjoyed his best year ever. At Suffolk I won a leading-rider award for the third time in less than twelve months and, generally, things were starting to happen. 1960 was Olympic year, but I felt it was most unlikely that I would get into the team, however well my bay horse was going, for Colonel Talbot-Ponsonby was in charge and Arundel had shown me that he did not go for my style of riding. Yet Farmer's Boy was of Olympic standard and whatever course was put up he would always come out at the other end. At combinations nothing could live with him and John Walmsley's Nugget. The thirty classes he won that season included the Area International Trial at Liverpool, in which Franco was second. Franco, I think, won only one or two Opens before going to Rome where his inexperience was fully exposed.

I remember I had an eventful time at the Bakewell (Derbyshire) Show the country's biggest one-day show. Farmer's Boy hit a pole in the collecting ring and a wing of the fence flew up and cracked me across the nose, breaking it. I was due in the ring straight away for the Grades A and B contest and we got third place. By the time the area trial began, half an hour later, the bleeding had stopped. When I get a knock like that and it seems the odds are against me, it usually has the effect of raising my performance. So it was that day, for Farmer's Boy won the competition. I did not bother to have my nose seen to and was none the worse for not doing so.

That season, I seemed to invite accidents. Later the same August another mishap occurred with Farmer's Boy during the Test at the British Timken, at Dunston. Halfway through the first round the strap pulled out of the saddle top and I had to free the saddle and let it drop. We completed the course without fault and, being a bit quiet in those days, I did not try to borrow another saddle. Consequently, I jumped another two rounds bareback, with the wall ending up at 6 feet 6 inches, and managed fourth place. As I always had ridden a lot without a saddle at home since my early gymkhana days the exercise was not too difficult.

Once you have ridden bareback you never forget. When it comes to the bareback class which now has become part of the Dunhill Show before Christmas you see some top international riders trying to practise but never going in the ring. I find it unbelievable how many of the good riders can't go without a saddle.

During that season we really mastered the art of converting the wagon into a temporary home. Once we had arrived at a show, we cleaned out the wagon, put a carpet down, installed a sink unit and a Calor gas stove, and put up a bed in the recess on top of the cab: it was just as good as a caravan and not at all the straw and horsemuck job which some people seemed to imagine.

The next year, 1961, was different in that Irene gave up her job as groom in favour of one as mother, our first son, Robert, being born in the June. They had just left the nursing home and gone to Irene's mother's when I journeyed up to Edinburgh for the Royal Highland. My anxiety in wanting to get back to them as quickly as possible once the show was over led me to push on a bit and I made good progress until well beyond Beattock summit in South Lanarkshire.

A young lad called William Halliday had made the trip with me and he had just gone into the back to make a sandwich or two when a front wheel came off and the wagon tripped over into the middle of the road. There was no sound from Montana and Farmer's Boy as I clambered out of the cab but as soon as I opened the door at the back they both greeted me with a whinny. They were on their sides with the gas stove, the pots and pans and Willie on top of them. He was unhurt and quite calm and we quickly cleared the stuff off first one and then the other, got them out of the wagon and turned them out in a field by the roadside.

A slight scratch on Farmer's Boy's neck was the only sign that they had been in trouble. It was a very lucky escape for all of us. The horses were saved, I think, by the fact that they had been travelling side by side without partitions between them. Had there been partitions up they would have been goners.

The cause of the trouble was a broken kingpin, which had let the wheel slip off the axle. The broken wagon was one we had converted and it had started out as a haulage vehicle for ovens. It was the successor to an ex-Burton's tailors van, on which my brother John and I also had done a conversion job. New wagons were far too expensive for me in those days and had not John and I been able to carry out all maintenance and repairs ourselves I could not possibly have afforded to break into show-jumping.

Generally, 1961 was another good year for Farmer's Boy and Montana. I paid my first visit to the All England Jumping Course at Hickstead and found it totally different from all other English courses. There were ditches, water under fences, a 'tennis court' and, of course, the now famous Hickstead bank. The first time I met this, on Farmer's Boy, it felt like going off the top of a double-decker bus. I did not form any preconceived notions of how to tackle it, but it caused no bother at all to my horse: he just went to the edge and slid down.

Not that the Hickstead bank is a favourite obstacle of mine. To my mind, it belongs to the realms of eventing, not show-jumping, and it is included purely as an attraction for the spectators. One or two horses have broken their pelvises on it and when a horse tells me, as War Paint did on one later occasion, that he does not fancy the prospect of descending the bank, I am quite content to back up his judgement.

It was in the autumn of 1961 that I bought War Paint. To start at the beginning, I was looking through the 'for sale' columns of *Horse and Hound* when I noticed that he was to be auctioned at Leicester. I had heard many people say what a good horse he could be if he hadn't such a bad stop, and I had also heard that he was foul-tempered. His early days had been spent in Leicester before he was sold to Leonard Cawthraw, owner of the legendary Pegasus, for Ted Williams to ride.

Later he was passed on to a girl and within a year of her getting him War Paint had become too clever for her. She asked Ted to get him going again and he was delivered to him for that purpose. On the first day Ted took him into the paddock and got him to jump a few fences; on the second day War Paint looked at the paddock and refused to enter; and on the third day he would not even go down the lane leading to the jumps. To make matters worse, he behaved viciously. Ted had too many good horses around the place to spare the time to attempt to cure War Paint and so he sent him back to his owner.

In due course he was sold again and Paddy McMahon took over as his jockey. All went well for a short time before he again chucked it up and then he was passed on yet again, this time to Christine Ash. She hunted him and got in a few shows in the year she had him before sending him to Leicester Sales. By then he was set in the habit of pulling up in the corners and refusing to budge. Some of these facts I learned after I had bought him, though had I known the lot I should still have gone after him. I had seen him jump some good fences, I knew he was sound and I knew that the little bit of noise he made in his wind did not bother him. Also on the credit side was that he had a mind of his own. If I could get his mind working my way then I would really have something. Down at the sale I could see that he was not going to be bought in the ring and he duly failed to reach his reserve. I spoke to Christine afterwards and she refused to take less than £300 – and what a bargain he turned out to be.

But first there was a battle of wills. When I took him out for the first time at home he dug in his toes and refused to go in the direction I wanted him to. I was on his back for six hours, during which time my wife Irene brought me a cup of tea. By the end of the sixth hour I had straightened him out. Far from being any more trouble, he became virtually the family pet as well as one of the top few jumpers in the country and a quarter of the best team I have ever travelled at any one time. The point is that you can ruffle a horse once to let him know who is boss but then you must kid him along so that he thinks, 'Oh well, he is not too bad; I'll go along.' If you go on ruffling him, he will get confused and fussed.

I always put myself in the horse's place. They are not unintelligent animals. If they are prepared thoroughly for what they are going to be asked to do, they will do it. But the request has to be one which makes sense. During one of the talk-ins and demonstrations which I give nowadays, I showed how I work my horses over cavaletti – at an angle sometimes, straight at others, and with the distances between them not uniform. The horse did everything right. 'Could you rein him back over them?' someone then asked. It was a silly question and the answer was that I would not try.

Putting myself in the horse's place does not mean that I get too familiar with him. That would be just as wrong as it would be for an employer to go out drinking with his workers. If an employer does that he is likely to finish up as an employee, with his men acting as the boss.

Returning to War Paint, I found that once I had gained his confidence he became the most gentle horse anyone could wish to have, in and out of the stable. Schooling him, we by-passed the small stuff and started at jumps of 4 feet and 4 feet 6 inches straight away. At the 1962 Royal International at the White City the following July he cleared 6 feet 11 inches to share the White Horse Whisky puissance with O'Malley and Dundrum, Tommy Wade's legendary half-Connemara pony.

War Paint began with me at Badminton in the spring of 1962 and jumped clear round after clear round. At those early shows people who had known him used to dash up to the ring, watch him do a good round and then say: 'Well, he was all right today but he will pack it in tomorrow.' He confounded them by winning good classes at Ascot, Badminton, the Bath and West and Oxford, and by finishing fourth in the Hickstead Derby.

They took heart, though, at the Shropshire County, a bad place for a horse which naps it and tries to get out of the job at hand. When taking a corner near the collecting ring on the first day, he very nearly stopped. Next day they were all there to watch him revert to his old behaviour and they were disappointed again. The idea that he could cheat on the corners, however, did stay with him.

By the time of the Royal Show, held at Newcastle that year and before it got a permanent home in Warwickshire, War Paint and Farmer's Boy were in grand form. Their performance could not be ignored by the selectors and shortly after the Royal I received a letter saying that I was invited to jump for Britain at the Royal International Horse Show at the White City – the first time I had been asked to do so since Dublin four years earlier.

The Royal was an eventful show for me because it was also there that Mr Robert Hanson first approached me about O'Malley, a brilliant Canadian horse which had jumped many times for his national team with Jimmy Elder. He was by Peepshow, an American thoroughbred, out of Willow, a Canadian half-bred hunter mare, and he was good-looking enough to win a good few breed classes in his in-hand days. Jimmy Elder soon upgraded him when he began jumping and O'Malley won the biggest competition at the Winter Fair in Toronto when he was only six. Mr Hanson was watching and persuaded his owner to part with him for what was then a very high price.

O'Malley was sent to Dick Stilwell, a professional horseman with stables at Windsor, on the understanding that he should have him until a suitable amateur was found. Being a professional, Dick Stilwell could not ride in Nations Cups and, of course, the Olympics were out for him. In the early months of 1962, O'Malley showed a lot of promise without winning much and I had a good look at him at Ascot.

From the ground he looked to be a strong-minded, wilful fellow but I could see that he did not kick out the fences deliberately but rather because he was messing about, fighting for his head. When Mr Hanson mentioned the horse to me at the Royal we arranged that I should have a sit on O'Malley the day before the Great Yorkshire at Harrogate the next week to see what Mr Hanson thought of me as O'Malley's rider and what I thought of O'Malley. I made the short journey from Gilstead to Harrogate on the appointed day and found that Mr Hanson had put up two or three fences in the car-park and I popped O'Malley over these. It does not take long to get the feel of a horse and those few jumps told me what I virtually knew already: that the horse was headstrong, yet full of courage and ability. Mr Hanson seemed satisfied at the way the horse had gone for me and asked if I would ride him at the show.

On the first day O'Malley had eight or twelve faults, running on and kicking the fences down, and on the second day just got in at the tail-end of the placings. He returned to Dick Stilwell's place after the show and I picked him up from there to take him to Liverpool, the intention being that I should get a really good feel of him before the White

City. He was well in the money, finishing second in the championship under Mr Hanson's gaze, and a contract then was produced for me to sign. It was to the effect that I should have the horse until after the 1964 Olympic Games in Tokyo, that Mr Hanson couldn't take the horse from me and that I could not push him back at Mr Hanson.

It was the first and last such contract for me. The basis of all owner-rider partnerships must be that the rider has an absolutely free hand. It is impossible to get the best out of a horse if the owner repeatedly is telling the rider when and where to jump. Say, for instance, that a good horse goes badly one day and a rider decides to put him in a little speed event. The owner's feelings might be that the rider had gone off his head and he possibly would argue that this was not the way to get the horse's confidence back. If the rider believes that the speed outing will do the trick then he must have absolute freedom to test his theory. The rider has enough to think about getting his horses ready without owners becoming involved in decisions. I was lucky in that my views were respected by most owners I rode for before, as a matter of policy, I stopped riding other people's horses. I got on well with Bert Cleminson, who sent Harvester to me in 1963, and George Thackray, part-owner with me of War Paint, Montana and Montana's successor, Sea Hawk, could not have been better.

After Liverpool, O'Malley joined War Paint and Farmer's Boy for the journey to the White City, the most exhausting show of the season. A normal day's routine there could be: out early for a class starting at nine a.m., lunch in the caravan or box, back in the ring straight afterwards for a second class, and then out again in the evening for a competition which might drag on until near midnight. Except for the meal arrangements, being in the national team was little different from previous visits as an individual competitor. It is difficult to create a strong team feeling at home shows.

Nat Kindersley was chef d'équipe, as he had been in Dublin, and it was he who approached me rather hesitantly

B

on Nations Cup day and, as tactfully as he could told me that I would not be in the team. I meant it when I replied: 'That is the best news I have had all day.' Not because I was feeling unpatriotic but because torrential rain had reduced the arena to a paddy-field.

Nevertheless, O'Malley or War Paint should have been in the team if the selectors had known their form. O'Malley showed them up in no uncertain manner in the John Player Trophy. After the two rounds into which this major competition is divided had taken place only O'Malley and Posillipo, ridden by Raimondo d'Inzeo, survived. I chose to have a real go and it came off. That was the first time I had really roasted the top internationals in a class that mattered.

Now all the riders had to respect my horses – a far cry from the mid-fifties. One incident sticks in my mind in this connection. Some of the top boys had come up for Blackburn Show and when it came to a jump-off they followed the usual practice at that time of dividing up the money before they went into the ring, so assuring themselves of a fixed return. They ignored me altogether. When they did not even ask me if I wanted to divide I knew they were not going to get the money at all. Farmer's Boy saw to it that they did not have much to divide up.

The practice did not appeal to me anyway. In the fifties some of the riders even used to pre-divide their Horse of the Year pickings, an arrangement which occasionally ended in ill-feeling when a rider who had won more than his share forgot the original agreement. It needed only a few incidents like that to convince riders that it was best to rely on their own ability.

After the White City I was nominated as a member of the team for Dublin, taking O'Malley and Montana. With the exception of France, we were the smallest team numerically. Judy Crago, with her recent Queen Elizabeth Cup winner, Spring Fever, Lady Sarah Fitzalan Howard with Oorskiet and the new European champions, David Barker and Mister Softee, were the other members.

It was by no means so successful a show as on my initiation four weeks earlier, although all the horses went fairly well and the week itself was enjoyable, as Dublin always is. The social round at Dublin demands a certain degree of abstinence. Those riders who take full advantage of their hosts' hospitality can easily be identified by a glance at the results later in the week when the pace is beginning to tell. The programme lined up for us in 1962 gives an idea of the care the Royal Dublin Society takes to see that visiting teams are given a good time. It went like this: Saturday – Leopardstown Races; Sunday – Royal Dublin Society at home; Monday – 2.30 p.m. Baldoyle Races, 6 p.m. after-the-races cocktail party, 11 p.m. Kildare Hunt Cotton Dance; Tuesday – 12.30 p.m. show luncheon, 8 p.m. dinner at McKee Barracks, 10 p.m. Tipperary Hunt Ball; Wednesday – 12.30 p.m. show luncheon, 10 p.m. choice of two balls; Thursday – 12.30 p.m. show luncheon, 6 p.m. cocktail party, 10 p.m. South County Dublin Hunt Ball, 11 p.m. Meath Hunt Ball; Friday – 12.30 p.m. show luncheon, 10 p.m. choice of two balls; Saturday – 12.30 p.m. final show luncheon.

You can see where the stamina comes in. And, of course, we have to do a bit of show-jumping as well.

From Dublin, after a brief stop-over in England, I left for my first Continental show, at Rotterdam. By this time, Farmer's Boy was slipping into the background, although he had a good year, winning or being placed forty-seven times, and on his day he could still best the best. His legs began to trouble him and sometimes he was a little stiff in the mornings until he had walked around for a while. I have heard it said that the unnerving operation can leave horses with a tendency to stumble but that certainly was not the case with Farmer's Boy.

With my travelling increasing and my time more taken up with jumping, I took on a full-time groom, Doreen 'Blossom' Bennett. For years she travelled all over the Continent with the horses as well as helping greatly with the novices and the general running of the stable.

Everything about the Rotterdam Show impressed me

favourably and made me keen on jumping on the Continent. The Dutch were excellent hosts, food and accommodation were good and the show was held in a lovely park.

O'Malley was in his element. Some thoughtful person added up the number of fences he jumped during the show and it came to 112. Of these, he had only one down and that in the final barrage of the puissance, when the wall just caught him at 6 feet 10 inches. He shared second place in that class with War Paint and Dundrum, behind Ferdl, ridden by Alwin Schockemohle who was just becoming a major force on the international circuit.

Alwin is still a great rival and friend. I have never seen a better rider when it comes to winning competitions, even if for a long while he just missed out in European and world championships. He is always grinding at you and he always has plenty of good horses. He is a top-class rider in his own right, but he also has the good fortune to have the horses to match his own ability while the top English riders often are taking him on with inferior horses.

The course-builder at Rotterdam was Jan Jurgens, regarded by many people at that time as perhaps the best in the world. He had the habit of making the courses too long and too easy and in the Grand Prix no less than twenty-one of the forty-six starters went forward to the jump-off against the clock. O'Malley was one of the first to go and, as in the John Player, we had a real cut. He did not make a semblance of a mistake and clocked a time which none of the others could get near. The prize included a ten-day cruise, the tickets for which I gave to Irene's mother.

Wembley 1962 was Farmer's Boy's last show. I turned him out at George Thackray's farm that winter and he did not come back quite as he should have done when I began his 1963 preparation. Had I not had so many good ones coming on I would have persevered but, as it was, I let him stay out at grass all that summer. His legs got worse and he aggravated matters by being the hero with the other horses and getting into tussles from which he always came out second best. By Wembley time he was so lame that I decided the only thing to do was to have him put down and I arranged for the knacker to drop him in his field as he was having a feed. I am not a sentimentalist in anything, yet I feel there might be a link between the old horse's departure and my poor Wembley that year.

Montana also left me that Wembley. Despite a record week, in which he won two of the three competitions in which I rode him and was second in the other, his legs weren't right. The ground had begun to stop him. George Thackray, who was then his owner, thought it best that neither of us should keep a horse who was not comfortable unless it was easy going, and I agreed.

In addition to Montana's two victories, War Paint won the Beaufort Stakes, the first of the meeting for the international horses, and shared the White Horse puissance with O'Malley and Dundrum. In the third barrage there was an oxer at 6 feet and the wall at 6 feet 11 inches. It was the highest O'Malley had ever been, although I knew he could do it, and both he and War Paint cleared the fences easily. Dundrum was just as comfortable, though, so Tommy Wade and I opted to divide rather than go on and risk frightening or injuring one of the horses.

Montana was sold on the Thursday night and on the Friday, looking for a horse to replace him in speed events, I spoke to Peter Robeson about Sea Hawk and quickly completed a deal, George Thackray and I both adding a bit of money to the £300 realized with Montana. Sea Hawk was not jumping at the show and, like War Paint, his career had been a mixture of good and bad, latterly mostly bad.

A grey, he was South-African bred, by a thoroughbred stallion called Dust-a-Blowing out of a thoroughbred mare. As a young horse he had won several hack classes and championships and later he came over to this country with Bob Grayston. I saw him jump a good round in the King George V Cup at the White City and he went down in my mind as a good mover who ate up the ground without seeming to be going at all. He did not achieve a lot with Bob Grayston and was sold to Peter.

They did not get on and Sea Hawk had hardly won a bean with Peter when I made my offer. I picked the horse up on my way home from Wembley and a fortnight later took him with me to Amsterdam and Brussels.

Back at Gilstead in that fortnight I put him over a lot of little fences to restore his confidence. I found that at first he would not go within thirty yards of a fence and to me this was a good fault. When horses do this it boils down to the fact that they prefer to chuck it up well away from the fence rather than hit it. Such horses are far better than careless ones; they are not going to have fences down, and all I have to do is keep them going forward.

When some riders are on a horse which stops they are so busy trying to stay on that they forget that punishment is due and that is when the horse begins to get his own way. If one stops with me, the moment he starts pulling up I let him know he has done wrong. If children are awkward with you they make not only you but also themselves miserable. It is just the same with horses. Let them know what you want, and that you want it done quickly, see that they do as they are told and then they will realize that they are right with you, you are right with them and the world is a lot happier place. It did not take Sea Hawk long to decide that if he was going to get his backside smacked for stopping he wasn't going to bother to stop and within a few days he was meeting the bigger stuff. Not that he ever became the bravest.

He was brilliant when things were going his way but the minute he hit a pole and hurt himself he went chicken-hearted on me. This did not prevent him winning at every international show he went to. He was only 15.2 hands or so but could really gallop fast and jump the fences as he galloped. He would go down as the best speed horse I have ever ridden and one of the very best show-jumping has ever seen.

I was not really fair to him in taking him over to the Continent so soon after getting him. I should have given him more time to build up because he had been turned out

down south and really was not fit and well as he should
have been. To begin with, he was too frightened to open
himself out when jumping. In his first competition at the
first show on the short tour – Brussels – his windiness caused
him to get a pole between his front feet and over he went.
He got in the money a bit in other classes without achieving
anything special.

The show, held in the Palais des Sports, lasted five days
and on every one of them there were capacity houses. As
on my trip a couple of months earlier, I found Continental
show officials to be tremendously helpful and cars were
laid on for the British team of Judy Crago, Pat Smythe and
myself. Pat had joined us from Madrid where she had won
the European Ladies' Championship.

With Sea Hawk not being ready and War Paint touching
the odd fence it was not a brilliant show for me but it was
educational and I was glad to see that the course-builder
Jean Legard, kept the speed courses big enough.

If the jumping did not provide me with much excitement,
the Brussels population did for the Flemish riots took place
the weekend before the show. When the Belgians get excited
they do it in style and it staggered me to see a crowd tipping
a tram straight over. As though this was not enough, the
Cuba crisis came to the boil and rumours were rife that
President Kennedy was going in. We had visions of having
to dash across the Channel but things died down and we
made our way to Amsterdam for the three-day international
show in the Nieuw RAI, generally known as 'the Rai'. This
is just about the finest indoor stadium one could wish for:
the ring is big, there is plenty of room in the collecting ring,
there are stands for the spectators and the stabling is under
the same roof. We in Britain have always been miles behind
when it comes to indoor jumping and, with the exception
of Wembley – which doesn't compare well with the Rai –
there is not a stadium which would make a national, never
mind international, indoor show. What we need is a pro-
moter with the good sense to see that there is good money
to be earned from indoor jumping.

Wembley is always booked solid before it opens. Britain has long needed a show-jumping circuit to follow on after Wembley taking in, say, Birmingham, Leeds and Glasgow. The top riders could be encouraged to stay over and I am positive that out of the millions who watch the Horse of the Year Show on television many thousands would grab the chance of seeing the big names in the flesh.

Amsterdam went well, largely due to War Paint, and I returned home having gained a real insight into the Continental scene. My mind was made up that I would get my full share of it from then on.

5. Harvester

I kept Sea Hawk up all the winter of 1962–3, riding him all over the moors and jumping everything we came across – walls, ditches, fallen timber – and then I took him and a novice or two down to the pre-season fixture at the Warwickshire Equestrian Club's place at Balsall Common, near Kenilworth. Sea Hawk won a couple of classes and they tuned him up nicely for the start of what was to be my best season to date.

Apart from Sea Hawk, the others in my string spent the winter at George Thackray's farm at Harewood, between Harrogate and Leeds. The horses there were turned out night and day, George feeding them twice in the twenty-four hours, and they benefitted in several ways. It gave them a chance to feed and think for themselves, for example, and also stopped them from getting soft. Animals which spend pampered lives do not have the necessary resistance when there are infections about.

At the end of January in 1963 War Paint and O'Malley were brought back to Gilstead and Doreen and I began to get them ready for the season ahead. Straight away they were put on hard grub and for three weeks or so they had ninety minutes a day on the moors, walking and trotting. before I switched them to faster work. This is the procedure I always follow. By the time the big competitions start they are as fit as racehorses, and that is the way I like to keep them. I do not ask them to do much jumping at home, limiting their schooling to two or three goes over a line of four fences or so.

That year we began at the Taunton Jumping Festival, over the Easter weekend. On the first day Sea Hawk won his

class and O'Malley was runner-up to Mr Pollard in the
Pollard Championship, the show's most valuable event.
O'Malley went one better the next day in the Simpson
Championship, Sea Hawk brought his score to two out of
two and War Paint got into the act by beating Merely-a-
Monarch in the Victor Ludorum, with O'Malley third. Sea
Hawk later completed his hat-trick by going too fast for
David Broome's Wildfire and Pam Harrison's Donner in
the Calypso Stakes and a novice, Springbok, made my total
six wins in a Grade C competition.

Earlier I had been notified that I was in the British team
for Rome, from 11 to 19 May, and after Taunton I was able
to fit just a few shows in before flying out from London
Airport. Irene also made the trip, as it seemed a good idea
to accept the chance of spending ten days in Rome together.
There were twelve horses on board the aircraft with the
team. I had three – O'Malley, Sea Hawk and War Paint –
Peter Robeson had Firecrest and Barsac, David Broome
took Wildfire and Lirep, David Barker, in addition to Mister
Softee, had another Massarella horse, Yorkshire Relish, Pat
Smythe took two already very well-known on the Continent,
Flanagan and Scorchin, and Anneli Drummond-Hay made
up the party with Merely-a-Monarch. We loaded the horses
ourselves and were on hand to deal with any trouble during
the flight. Two or three horses who were thought likely
to be bad travellers were given a tranquillizing shot before
we took off and I was asked to allow O'Malley to be injected. He may be an excitable kind of horse but he is not
short of common sense, so I refused. They need not have
worried for he behaved perfectly all the way, whereas those
who had been tranquillized caused the most bother of all. We
arrived two days before the start of the show in order to
give the horses a chance to settle down in the warmer climate
and this proved quite long enough.

The home of the show, the Piazza di Siena, is a beautiful
place and the ring itself lies at the bottom of a natural, tree-
lined arena. There is no end of room for schooling and all
the facilities are first rate. The horses were stabled in the

military barracks in the city some three miles from the stadium.

Everything considered, I felt there was no reason why the team should not do well against the hot competition we were going to be faced with from teams representing Germany, France, Russia, Ireland, Spain and Romania. Not forgetting the host nation whose team included the d'Inzeo brothers and the impressive Graziano Mancinelli. The only slightly disturbing thing so far as I was concerned was a niggling pain in my back, though that did not worry me much, at first.

Sea Hawk picked up where he had left off at home by beating Raimondo d'Inzeo's Merano in the Premio Pincio and as Merano was at that time the top speed horse in the world this result confirmed for me that my grey also ranked as one of the leading half-dozen in speed events.

But for an unfortunate incident, he should also have had first place in the Premio Generale Piero Dodi, in which officially he was placed third to Nelson Pessoa's Cangaceiro and a Romanian, V. Pinciu, on Classic. In this competition points are scored for each fence cleared, and I knew that in adding up Sea Hawk's score the judges had missed one fence out and the German chef d'équipe was among several other people to spot their mistake. He very kindly approached Colonel Nat Kindersley, our manager, and told him that he would go with him to the judges, point out their error and try to get the result corrected. Colonel Kindersley would have none of it – presumably such an appeal conflicted with his views on sportsmanship and the British attitude of being a good loser. I was not pleased. After all, be a good loser if you have lost, not if you have won. I have no time for the old-school-tie routine of smiling and accepting mistakes gracefully. I was not in a position to do anything about that particular case, but the chef d'équipe's first job should, I feel, be to look after the interests of his team and he should have seen that I got my proper reward.

I had first seen Nelson at the White City six or seven years earlier and he had built up a tremendous reputation, especially since setting up base in Geneva each summer in order to concentrate on the Continental circuit. He is always worth watching and I came to regard him as clearly the world's greatest rider indoors. His horses usually are small, sharp and lithe, just like cats, and Nelson is very quick-witted himself, so that they excel in the indoor rings where things happen very quickly. Outside Nelson is not effective in the same way and he is just average as international riders go. The reason is that there is more distance between the fences out of doors and he is not able to keep his horses going in the same sweet way. Of course, he wins his share of prizes and is always a rider to contend with.

The Gran Premio di Roma, the Grand Prix, was the main individual competition and eleven European nations were represented. Things looked promising for Britain after the first round, Mister Softee, Merely-a-Monarch, Scorchin and O'Malley having gone clear, but Hans Winkler was still there on Romanus, so was Piero on a youngster, Damigella, and, most dangerous of all to my mind, there remained Kif-Kif, bought by the Spanish government from Paco Goyoago for £20 000 and still ridden by him. Kif-Kif, a polo pony type standing only 15.2 hands, could just about fly. He could really gallop, stand off his fences, turn, get height and width – in fact, he did everything and he was bang on form.

David Barker was first to go on Mister Softee. I was told later that he had been instructed by the chef d'équipe to go for a good clear round with a view to putting the pressure on the non-British horses, so leaving the way clear for Anneli, Pat or myself to step in and clinch things. I was not aware of this at the time and David did not exactly coast along on the way to a second clear round. Anneli and Monarch then jumped one of their best rounds to go into the lead before Piero had one down. It had developed into a really hot class. With Anneli's brilliant time to beat and Kif-Kif to follow I knew O'Malley was going to have to pick up vital fractions of a second somewhere and decided that the place was between the water and a big parallel in the centre of the ring. O'Malley had no trouble with the first fence, cleared the water well and I then sent him flat out at the parallel. He met it on a good long stride, picked up and jumped it, and by so doing won the Grand Prix. Kif-Kif just failed to catch us, though he squeezed Monarch out of second place, Romanus was too slow to get in the picture and Scorchin moved up into fourth position with a good clear.

Mr Hanson was there to see O'Malley's triumph and receive the magnificent Romulus and Remus trophy which went with it. It was a moving moment for him because his late son William had been the last Englishman to win the Rome Grand Prix, ten years beforehand. As he had kept his son's trophy he allowed me to take the new one and it remained a valued possession of mine until I returned it to Mr Hanson, who needed it for one of his business offices.

A terrific downpour nearly caused a postponement of the puissance – show-jumping's high-jump competition – but the ground was just good enough for the competition to go on and it turned out to be a thriller. After three rounds four of us were still there: Raimondo d'Inzeo on Gowran Girl, Alwin Schockemohle on Ferdl and Hans Winkler on Fidelitas. Gowran Girl dropped out after the fourth leaving three to fight it out over a wall of 6 feet 7 inches and one of the biggest triples I have ever faced. Normally when puissances have got down to two fences you jump one going away from home, then turn and jump the stiff one (in most cases the wall) on the way back. This is not so in Rome where I found that the wall came first on the way out and the triple straight on. Horses tend to come home better than they go away, when often they hang a bit towards the collecting ring. Fidelitas was not good enough to clear either of the two in the final barrage and Ferdl faulted at the triple after clearing the wall. O'Malley also mastered the wall but toppled a pole off the triple to tie for first place. After this competition Ferdl proved himself to be the greatest puissance horse the world has ever seen, winning well over a hundred puissance competitions.

There were two other big events, the European Championship, decided in three stages, and the Nations Cup. In the European Championship Ireland took an early lead through Captain Billy Ringrose, and Loch an Espaig. Both at that time had been around for a while and both were top-class. They went really well here over the big speed course to finish ahead of Freiherr, a real good horse taken over by Alwin Schockemohle after getting the better of Reinata Freitag, and Mancinelli on Rockette, a first-rate speed horse. Riders can have only two horses in the championship and I opted for War Paint, rather than Sea Hawk, to partner O'Malley. Brilliant as he was against the clock in normal competitions, Sea Hawk was not much good when the fences were big. In addition, War Paint could move when I wanted him to. On this occasion he went well in hand to finish fourth. He could have gone a bit faster but would have stood a chance of having one down to do so. The second round was over a Nations Cup type course and I started War Paint again. He jumped one of only three clears to tie for first place with Mancinelli on The Rock and Alwin on Ferdl, so as we came to the final round I was third, behind Mancinelli and Alwin, and with a chance of the championship if I could win. This third round should have been held the day after the others but a thunderstorm flooded the place out and the rest day was brought forward to allow the sun to do its work.

I was not quite sure which horse to ride as the start of the final round drew near. War Paint was going so well, though, that my preference was for him. With him I could say: 'Today you are going to be brilliant, my lad,' and he would do his level best to see that he was brilliant. O'Malley, on the other hand, was that bit more brilliant on his day. The trouble was that I was never sure when that day was to be. Here at Rome he was, in any case, almost too well – jumping out of his skin, in fact. Nevertheless, I was persuaded to ride O'Malley, albeit against my better

judgement. I should not have allowed myself to be persuaded, for O'Malley, headstrong at the best of times, ran
on and jumped right in the middle of a couple of fences and
that was that so far as the championship was concerned.
Alwin did not do well either, whereas Mancinelli won on
Rockette and so was the overall winner. Alwin was runner-
up for the championship and I was third. I was pleased
enough to be third, considering that sixteen of the world's
top riders were competing.

Eight teams came out for the Nations Cup, ours consisting of Firecrest, Merely-a-Monarch, Mister Softee and
War Paint. Anneli was pleased to be number 16, the same
as when she had won the Badminton three-day event. She
is very superstitious, as is Renée Robeson, Peter's wife.
Neither of them will sit at a table at which thirteen places
have been set, for instance. They believe in good luck and
bad luck and when things are going their way they only
believe luck is working for them. With Anneli this means
that she really gets down to business with an extra bit of
confidence. The result here was that Merely-a-Monarch
jumped clear in both rounds and only one horse out of the
thirty-two equalled that feat.

Softee was also clear first time, Firecrest had two down
and War Paint one. This put us equal first place with the
Germans, on a four-fault total. Monarch's second clear was
matched by K. Jarasinski on Torro, but the Germans fell
behind when the best Romanus and Ferdl could do was to
have two down, whereas Firecrest had only one mistake.
As the fourth German, Ilona, notched up sixteen and Softee
only eight victory was ours before War Paint went in, with
a maximum total of sixteen compared with the twenty of the
Germans.

Third was an Italian team without Piero d'Inzeo, fourth
the Russians, who had won the Nations Cup in Paris and
astounded everyone by doing so. They had one or two good
horses but not enough to make a strong all-round team.

On the night before the show's final day the whole
British party, including Irene, paid a visit to a nightspot run

by a former ballet dancer well known to Anneli and her family. He had created a restaurant out of an ancient wine cellar and it had a marvellous atmosphere. A big open spit was in the centre and the waiters were all capable musicians and singers, as we found out after the meal was finished. David Barker had not had too good a show and we all decided that something had to be done. So I took him on in a little drinking match: as fast as he downed his wine I downed my drink, only mine was water. I was still going great guns when David got up feeling badly and retreated to the hotel. There was a happy sequel to all this when David won the show's final competition, the Prix Fulgosi, having nearly twelve seconds to spare over Hermann Schridde on Ilona in the jump-off.

During the show we had the usual Embassy reception to attend and, as ever, lots of well-meaning people did their best to chat us up. I remember there was one elderly lady who stunned me with questions about my forehand drive. The international tennis was on the same week and she had got it all wrong. And she wasn't the only pudding-head we met. Still, socially and otherwise, it was a good trip, marred for me only by the pain in my back which had grown worse each day, so that on the last couple of days I couldn't get on a horse without assistance and I needed lifting off, too.

I was worried at the prospect of having to rest just as the season was reaching its peak and I feared that I could be out of action for some time. Anneli came to the rescue by telling me of a Mr Rhodes Cook, a Harley Street physiotherapist and former Amateur Boxing Association area titleholder, to whose treatment a great many sportsmen were indebted, so I learned. I was a sorry sight as I went in to see him, as I could not straighten up at all. First, he arranged for X-rays to be taken. I went back the next day and he put me under anaesthetic before getting to work on my injured back. As soon as I came round I felt good and after a couple of manipulative sessions with him I was back to normal. The trouble has never recurred.

After landing back in London from Rome I sent the

horses on to Aldershot where I joined them after the treatment from Mr Rhodes Cook. Only two days went by, in fact, before I pulled O'Malley out and shared first place in the Southern Counties Championship on him. He went on in tremendous form, being thereabouts in nearly every class he entered, winning the £100 South Yorkshire Area International Trial at Wickersley, the big Open at the Northern Jumping Show at Wetherby – a show that does a very good job in raising funds for paralysed sportsmen and sportswomen – and then, in early July, landing the BSJA National Championship at Stoneleigh. War Paint was also going well, so that my own county show, the Great Yorkshire, found me having my best season ever.

The Great Yorkshire Show at Harrogate in 1963 was a good one for me in more ways than one. O'Malley won the three big competitions, War Paint being second in one and third in the other two, and I got to know Harvester. Bert Cleminson, a Rawcliffe man who turned out winner after winner in hunter classes and supplied hunters to many Masters of Foxhounds, had been on to me for several months saying what a good horse the young Harvester was and asking if I would have a sit on him. Bert, as usual, was at Harrogate and mentioned his horse to me again. I saw him go there at the end of the show, ridden by Bert's daughter, Carol, and half liked him. He was a big show horse, his actual height being 17 hands, but he moved better than most.

'Okay,' I said, 'I'll have a sit on him.' We played about for a while and jumped a plank 3 feet high or so, and then Bert went mad and raised it to 5 feet 6 inches. Harvester jumped this clean seven or eight times, really bending and using himself. 'Right, I'll take him,' I told Bert. Things happened so quickly that I think Bert was half stunned, for as soon as I got off the horse I had him loaded into my wagon and he was down at Hickstead jumping with me the next day.

In his first outing there he was third in a Grades B and C and next time out, again in a B and C, he won. After that

I let him have a look in the main ring, in one of the big competitions, and he won a small award. The way Harvester VI, to give him his full title, went spoke well for Carol. She had produced him in hunter and working hunter classes and he had beaten some good ones, especially when he became Working Hunter of the North at the Northern Horse Show. His first show-jumping class, as a five-year-old in 1961, was a Foxhunter at Holme-on-Spalding Moor, a village affair, and he got a third. The late Chris Jackson then rode him in two classes at another little show before Carol took over again. He won for the first time at Topcliffe, in July, earning £4 by doing so, and added four more victories in a light season which ended with a fourth in the Foxhunter regional final at Fairburn.

He was suspended after that because he had jumped in a Foxhunter when ineligible, a mistake which was very easily made. As a result, he did not come out until June in 1962. In a very brief season he won two classes at a small show near his stable, Huby and Sutton-on-Forest, one of them being a hit-and-hurry.

By 1963 he had developed well. He began by winning a strong B and C class at Wetherby and then won twice for Carol's friend, Angela Radcliffe, a girl who rode point-to-point horses for Bert and won the reputation of being one of the best riders in ladies' races before hurting her back badly in a race fall. Harvester, with Carol on board again, then won another strong B and C at the Northern Horse Show and a minor Open before his try-out with me at Harrogate. I liked his temperament. Only three parts thoroughbred, he was as honest as the day and not the least bit excitable. Ask him anything, and he would try to do it for you and, very important, he did not like to hit a fence. Hickstead was encouraging, and he went well enough after that at Liverpool, where I put him in the Open and won fourth prize. He then had a short break while I took the Grade A horses to the White City.

I left Harvester with my friend Jack White down at the Airedale Beagles' Kennels. He exercised him for me and kept him ticking on while I was at the Royal International. Jack was a very practical man, the sort you could put out on the moors in a tent, with only natural resources at his disposal, and who would manage to live really well. He could not go anywhere without rummaging round saddlers' shops, picking bits up and examining tack. Many a time he and I have sorted through his collection and used various parts to make a bit for one of my horses.

The point is that you cannot walk into a saddlers' shop and buy a bit of the exact type you need. Most of them are one and a half inches too big, for a start. I always try to make the bit fit the horse's mouth and not the mouth fit the bit. If a shoe is too big or too tight it is going to rub the wearer sore somewhere. So it is with a bit, only a horse's mouth is far more tender than a human's foot. Some riders are like butchers: they do not bother to see that the bit is comfortable and they are heavy-handed, too. I have seen horses coming out of the show-jumping ring with blood running from their mouths, and I would say that 60 per cent of show-jumpers are wrong in their mouths, either as a result of bad early education or ignorance on the part of the rider. Not that show-jumpers are the only ones to suffer. Many hunters and ordinary riding horses and ponies get ill-treated in the same way.

To make sure that horses' mouths do not get sore I make bits myself, sometimes cutting lumps out of the middle to shorten them up, sometimes making them narrower so that the finished article fits correctly and comfortably.

I took War Paint, O'Malley and Sea Hawk down to the White City. The Nations Cup had not been won in London by a British team for six years and the selectors chose Merely-a-Monarch, Mister Softee, Ann Townsend's promising Dunboyne III and War Paint to try to stop the rot. Italy, Ireland, France and Switzerland were in opposition. It was a one-horse race from the start but not without incident for me. War Paint was fourth to go in the first round and as we had a no-fault score when his turn came Colonel Kindersley told me: 'Do as you like; fall off if you like.'

'Okay,' I said. And I did – fall off, that is. I came around a corner a bit sloppy and my old fellow realized that I was just clowning and messing about. 'Right, my lad,' he thought to himself, 'you can have the school this time,' and he slapped me straight over some planks. I had been riding him so deep that he could not take off properly and rather than hurt himself he stopped and sent me straight on, which is what I deserved. Goodbye and Dundrum did well for Ireland but there was no strong support and we ran out easy winners with twelve faults to spare.

The White City over, I picked up Harvester and crossed over the Pennines to Blackpool for the Royal Lancashire Show, which featured that year the £500 Matthew Brown Trophy. War Paint, O'Malley and Harvester all shared sixth place, the £500 prize going to Sea Hawk who was letting them know that he could beat them at their own game.

Down south again, to the Ascot Jumping Show in which I started in eleven competitions and won eight of them. Harvester played his part by winning two and earning his biggest prize to date – £200 – for a third in the *News of the World* Championship. Sea Hawk was also in top form, winning on all four days, and O'Malley was at his brilliant best in the Michael Sobell Stakes and the Renault Grand Prix.

With the Grand Prix prize went a Renault estate car. Mr Hanson drove this round the ring in the lap of honour while I cantered O'Malley, and then I had a go at the wheel. I had never owned a car of my own and I was keen to have this one, so I paid Mr Hanson for his share and took it back with me to Bingley.

Wembley 1963 was not a good or happy one for me. The horses got places, Harvester being runner-up to Vibart in the Leading Show Jumper of the Year competition, but I didn't have a big win and the knockers got to work. Someone with a short memory wrote in the press that neither Sea Hawk nor War Paint were in the top international class. This sort of thing is not new. You have only got to slip a little and there is always someone eager to snipe at you. In later years after I had been on the North American circuit and won the New York Grand Prix, broken the Canadian puissance record with a jump of 7 feet 3 inches (on O'Malley) and been top international rider in Washington, one leading authority spread himself in the press to the effect that I could not be considered a good rider by international standards. You just cannot win.

In 1963 I was already beginning to have trouble with the press and this, to some extent, has continued to the present day. I do not enjoy reading about what I have done and in fact I have got to the point where I never read anything which is printed about me. This is because I have found that the press do not do me justice. They make up stories for their own ends. The simple truth would not be sensational enough for their editors or sports editors. Often someone comes up and tells me of a newspaper story about me. 'Look,' I'll say, 'there is nothing I can do to stop them printing such stories. Let them print what they like. It's just water off a duck's back to me.'

I have been accused of being suspicious of people. I'd say I was careful rather than suspicious. When you have been let down so many times by so many people you reach a stage where you dare not speak to the press. There have been times when I have done an article with a pressman and gone through it word for word with him afterwards. But it has been completely different from that when it has gone in his paper.

Such incidents don't worry me, they annoy me because I don't like lies. I'm down the line myself – if I say to someone that I will meet them at the North Pole at midnight on Christmas Eve I would be there at a minute to midnight. But too many pressmen treat the use of words as a game. Words do not have a true meaning to them.

There are some reporters I could trust with my life. There are others who are just little cheapjacks picking something out of nothing and blowing it sky-high. And even some of the better ones fall into the trap of condemning too much. The sport needs all the publicity it can get but not of the sensational kind. Too many show-jumping correspondents spend their time knocking the sport which is getting them a living when they should be helping it along.

Wembley 1963 also saw me involved in a row over the courses set by Lieutenant-Colonel Jack Talbot-Ponsonby. Everything about them was wrong, the distances being set on half-strides so that often it was impossible for the horses to make it. Foreign riders as well as British were rowing about them. I voiced the criticisms to Colonel Ansell. Later my invitation to jump with the British team in Geneva was withdrawn and it seemed to me that I was being made to suffer because I had opened my mouth and criticized the Horse of the Year Show. I found as the years went by that riders with a grievance were only too happy to let me do the unpleasant work by taking the complaints to authority and that, meanwhile, they were slipping off and stabbing me in the back.

The list of the season's Top Ten for competitions in this country showed O'Malley at the top, seven places higher than the year before. Sea Hawk was fourth, seventh was War Paint and Harvester had done very well to get in the list at the tail end.

After Wembley I spent just a few days with Irene and Robert in our new home, a semi-detached in Gilstead, backing on to the family firm's yard and just a short walk from my stable block. Then off again, this time to Amsterdam where I was the only British rider competing. It was a very enjoyable show, the Dutch once more being first-rate hosts, and it was an appropriate ending to as good a season as I could have wished for.

6. Olympic fiasco

Ahead lay Olympic year. The BSJA had a master plan for the 1964 Olympic Games to be held in Tokyo. Colonel Nat Kindersley was appointed team manager and his duties during the winter and early spring months were given out as 'being in contact with all horses and riders [in line for a place in the team] discussing the progress and training'. The new Olympic rule forbade a team to train collectively for more than three weeks so, even if the Association had wanted to, the short-list horses could not be brought together for a long spell of preparation. It was also stated that the selected riders should have ample opportunity to develop as a team 'able to share advice and criticism'. The second stage of the plan was to be a series of matches between Great Britain and the Rest, to find in competition which were the right horses for the job.

It all sounded reasonable enough in theory. In practice it was quite different. I, for one, never set eyes on Colonel Kindersley during the winter, although, I believe, the owners of two of my Olympic possibles, O'Malley and Harvester, did. There were attempts to get O'Malley for another international rider and I suspect that such was the case with Harvester, too. At the back of their minds was the fact that I am not interested in being regarded as a fine sportsman, only in winning: I believe a competitor's job is to win, not just to take part, and this attitude is not admired. So far as I was concerned, they were hardly going about things in the right way to encourage team spirit. The idea of holding Olympic trials was a good one, made useless by the nature of the courses set when the time came.

As the start of the season approached my mind was not on Tokyo but on doing as well as possible with all my horses. O'Malley had been turned out with the others at George Thackray's farm and was quite sound after sustaining a badly gashed leg the previous season.

The Royal Windsor, in mid-May, was chosen as the occasion for the first of the three Olympic trials, the original idea of having four or five having been changed. Three teams of four horses were chosen. David Barker on Mister Softee, Douglas Bunn on Beethoven, Andrew Fielder on Vibart and Julie Nash on Trigger Hill made up Wilf White's team; William Barker on North Flight, David Broome on Ballan Silver Knight, Anneli Drummond-Hay on Merely-a-Monarch and Peter Robeson on Firecrest, formed that under the name of Colonel Llewellyn; and Ann Townsend on Dunboyne, Pat Smythe on Flanagan, George Hobbs on Brandy Soda and myself on O'Malley were down as Lieutenant-Colonel D. N. Stewart's team. Lieutenant-Colonel Jack Talbot-Ponsonby built the course, supposedly based on that over which Britain won the team gold medal in Helsinki in 1952. Only it was modified to such an extent that it was nothing like Olympic proportions and was not a true test of a horse's ability.

Three of the horses jumped double clears – O'Malley, Vibart (who was not going to be able to go to Tokyo because Andrew was under the lower age limit) and Trigger Hill. Good horse that he is, Trigger Hill would not be able to jump a clear over an Olympic course. Others in the team were clearly not up to the job, among them Ballan Silver Knight. The selectors knew this and for some time had been fishing around to find an Olympic horse for David. Their gaze for a time focused on Vibart but Andrew, well within his rights, refused to hand his horse over. Vibart was a big, scopey horse, and just the type needed for the Olympic Games. He was not, though, the type of horse to suit David, who is best on the fluffy kind which goes bounding along within himself. Of course, he rode Sunsalve brilliantly, but Sunsalve was a freak. No nation ever has more than a handful of riders really fit to take part in the Olympics – Hans Winkler told me once that any nation with three such riders is lucky to the point of the miraculous – and the policy of trying to find a mount for David had some sense behind it. But however good a rider is he cannot make the grade without the right horse as the Olympic selectors discovered when they put him up on Jacapo for the Games.

In that first trial, apart from O'Malley, who played with the course, and Vibart, the performances of North Flight, Firecrest and Monarch were satisfactory, each having a combined total of four faults, and after a poor first round Mister Softee came back with a clear in the second. When the time came for the BSJA selection committee to nominate three teams for the second trial, at Wilmslow at the end of May, Monarch and Softee were out of action and Brandy Soda, Flanagan and Trigger Hill of the first-trial horses were not considered. They only just managed to scrape together three teams, giving the title of 'Great Britain' to that composed of Franco (David Barker), Firecrest and O'Malley. David Broome was in the 'probables' on an impossible, Deric, with David Boston Barker on his seven-year-old North Riding, David's brother, William, on North Flight, and Johnny Kidd on Copper Castle; while Vibart, who was not going to Tokyo whatever happened, led another team of so-called probables.

It might have been fun for the selectors, and it certainly drew the crowds, but that second Olympic trial was not of the slightest value. Vibart and Franco got double clears, O'Malley was clear first time and faulted only at the water in the second round and Firecrest, North Riding and Deric each had one clear. There simply was no point in holding a trial over such an easy course for it proved nothing. Our reward, by the way, for taking part at Wilmslow was a little ashtray.

In between Royal Windsor and Wilmslow my horses had been going well, but with Harvester an absentee. He joined me again in early June, too big and only half fit, and yet he quickly got into his stride.

So it went on through June, a highlight for me being the Gamblers Irish Sweep Stake at the Royal Highland, a show noted for the high all-round level of its prize money, for showing and show-jumping classes. The fences included a big drum with poles on top, which all the competitors jumped the easy way. Harvester was last to go and I jumped it with him both ways, again and again, and it got him first place. That competition came over so well on television that it is still recalled to me by people who saw it. There was no stopping Harvester. The Royal Norfolk Area International Trial, the Goathland Stakes at the Great Yorkshire, the Lancashire AIT at Liverpool, the Royal Lancashire Adult Championship, and the Whitbread Open at Bakewell all came his way, so that by early August he was well into four figures for his short season. And that was after being an onlooker at the Royal International at the White City.

Before the White City and immediately after the Royal Highland I went with the British team to Aachen. This was one of the foreign shows at which the short-list horses were supposed to prove themselves in good form for the battle ahead. Mister Softee, however, was having tendon trouble and was out of action and, though Merely-a-Monarch was selected he started going wrong, causing a good deal of concern to his rider, Anneli Drummond-Hay. The three Barkers were in the team, David with Franco and Beefeater, David Boston with North Riding and William with the best of the lot, North Flight, a very good mare who later developed into one of the best show-jumping mares in the world.

It was my maiden trip to Aachen and first impressions of the show were very favourable. The ring was very, very big, the organization was as efficient as anyone could wish and the setting was really lovely. The opening competition was a Grade A contest against the clock and Sea Hawk won it easily from Mlle Janou Lefebvre's Or Pailleur, another good speed horse. Sea Hawk won again on the fourth day of the nine-day show, again having plenty of time to spare over the second horse in a doubles and trebles for which there were seventy-four starters. At both indoor and outdoor shows in Germany there are nearly always too many for comfort, principally because they have so many good-quality jumpers over there. Even in the huge fields there are few passengers.

There were fifty-four forward for a big Table A a couple of days later but the tricky going reduced this to seven, the only British survivor being War Paint. He went clear second time, too, to give him first place with Raimondo d'Inzeo on Bells of Clomwell, Alwin Schockemohle on Freiherr and another German, P. Schmitz on Monodie. And that was it for me and for the team at Aachen. We did not win another thing. O'Malley got near enough and was jumping everything but the water. He got it into his head that he was not going to jump it and he didn't. He knew that he could not hurt himself at it and so slopped over it. Not that he went into the water; he would jump a yard over and then put his foot back on the tape. What he wanted was the tape to jump up and wrap itself round his neck! Put him to water at home and he would give it two yards to spare every time. Which all goes to show that horses are cute.

The only teams behind us in the Nations Cup were the Swiss and the Russians, the latter knocking up a cricket score. It had begun to look as though we were falling back as an Olympic force and the selectors appeared to panic. If only they had kept their heads I feel sure we would have been in the medals in Tokyo; and that Britain did so badly was, I think, their fault and not the fault of the competitors or the horses.

After Aachen I had a good time at the Great Yorkshire, where War Paint and Harvester won the big competitions on the first two days and O'Malley was second to Firecrest in the championship on the third, and then made my way to the White City. As this is an international event, I was allowed only three horses so, although I took Harvester down just in case, he waited on the sidelines all week and did not turn out. There was trouble straight away. It was stated that Merely-a-Monarch had been placed by Mr Hanson under the jurisdiction of the Olympic selection committee and that David Broome was going to be his partner from then on. They got together for the first time in the Nizefela Stakes but the experiment did not continue and the Broome in the Nations Cup was Elizabeth, on Jacapo, not David. The course for it was a small one containing nothing to make a horse jump at all. There were things in it which a 14.2 hands pony could have cleared. Firecrest, Jacapo and North Riding had double clears for us while in the first round O'Malley put a foot on the water tape and had a little four-feet job down. There was no need for him to go again.

It all looked good on paper, with the Italians second, the Americans third and Ireland fourth but really it was valueless. Elizabeth raised a lot of hopes by winning the Lonsdale Championship, the puissance, on Jacapo. There were a lot of good horses behind them and this led to Elizabeth's making way later for her brother and to Jacapo's being chosen for Tokyo. Yet the Lonsdale was not a true puissance, heights were not well up and it was sloping poles which caused most of the trouble.

The British Timken on 28 and 29 August had been chosen as the venue for the third and final Olympic trial and, as it approached, pessimism and panic got a grip on the selectors. According to influential critics, O'Malley was not only unsound but stale as well – and evidently the selectors took their word for it. Certainly no selector got in touch with me at any time to ask how O'Malley was and what my plans with him were, and none of the selectors had put in enough travel during the season to know how the 'possibles' were or were not. My cause had not been helped, by the way, when I had had a bit of a dust-up with Colonel Kindersley at Aachen. It was something and nothing about a parade; I think I had taken the horses away at the wrong time, but my chances of Olympic selection were perhaps not helped by not seeing eye to eye with the Colonel.

Still, I did find myself in the Great Britain team for the

final Olympic jumping trial on the Saturday at Duston, Northamptonshire. I was on War Paint and the others in the team were Peter Robeson and Firecrest, David Boston Barker and North Riding, and David Broome on Jacapo. Teams of Senior Internationals and Young Internationals opposed us, the seniors being Fred Welch on Brule Tout, Judy Crago on Spring Fever, George Hobbs on Brandy Soda and Alan Oliver on Galway Bay. William Barker and North Flight stood out as the best combination in the younger team, in which there were also Valerie Clark and Atalanta, Janet Smith with Silver Toes and John Kidd on Copper Castle.

A better course was built this time, although still not a testing enough one for the job it was supposed to do. We ended up in front of the youngsters, for whom North Flight had a good round. Of course, the result of the trial was of no importance in that its supposed purpose was to find four horses who would best represent Great Britain in Tokyo; or at the very least it was intended to help the selectors in making their choice. But what happened? As soon as the trial was over the selectors named Peter as team captain for Tokyo. Yet only one horse out of the eleven who completed two rounds incurred more faults than Firecrest. There simply was no logic in their action. The selectors also announced that two of the three remaining places would go to North Riding and Jacapo.

My opinion of Jacapo has already been given: not a bad horse but not within a mile of being an Olympic one. North Riding was inexperienced and inconsistent. He could go out and jump some really good rounds. He could go out, too, and jump some really bad ones. Above all, what is needed for courses like those met in the Olympics is a consistent horse. The one place was left, so it was said, so that Mister Softee or O'Malley would have a chance to prove their fitness. If anyone had asked me I could have told them that O'Malley would be right again in plenty of time, but they did not ask and William Barker was later chosen to join his elder brother in the team with North Flight. Harvester, who was quite sound and a true Olympic horse, was not even considered and War Paint was ruled out. And War Paint was the one horse with tremendous scope, a very big jump and no problem fence; he was the horse who could have won the individual gold medal.

So, controversially, I was out of the Games which, as it turned out, were not a happy event for the British team – they returned empty-handed from Tokyo.

Later in the year at the Horse of the Year Show O'Malley was back on good form. He was thereabouts on every single day of the show – and was supposed to be stale and unsound. War Paint showed how well he was going by winning the *Sunday Times* Cup from Goodbye and the top twelve horses in Britain.

At the beginning of 1965 I had the stables down behind the yard pretty well filled with good horses. There were the old-stagers, War Paint and Sea Hawk, both still in their prime, O'Malley, Rolling Hills and Harvester, who came back from Bert's earlier than usual with a view to kicking off at Badminton in April. When Mr Hanson originally bought O'Malley in Canada and brought him over to this country I believe the horse at first failed his veterinary examination because of a slight defect in his wind. It had never bothered him, though I had noticed in 1964 that he was starting to flag at the end of a course, especially if the weather was hot. Because of this I took him down to the hobday expert, Colonel Townsend, for the operation. It was entirely successful and he was perfect in his wind from that day on. I never even considered having the horse tubed, because I would not travel one with such a thing in his throat.

So, springtime came with all well at Gilstead. Doreen was doing her usual job and all the horses were fit and well, none more so than O'Malley. I had him entered for some shows, and the first was only a fortnight or so away when the unexpected happened in a big way. It all began quietly enough when Mr Hanson rolled into the yard one day, had a look at his horse, and then just said: 'By the way I will want an increased share of the prize money this year.'

'You know that's impossible,' I replied.

'Well, I'll leave him for a fortnight for you to think it over,' Mr Hanson added.

It was no use thinking it over and I had to tell him so. 'The job doesn't tie up as it is,' I pointed out, 'so it is no use my thinking about it.'

Mr Hanson was silent for a while and then said nothing more, other than 'All right', before driving off.

That night I talked about the incident to Irene and we decided that on the basis that Mr Hanson had suggested we simply would have no chance of covering expenses. And just in case it is thought that riders with other people's horses are on to a good thing I shall emphasize that it is the rider who has to pay for fuel for the wagons, and wagon maintenance and repair, and also the rider who has to pay the grooms, pay the feed and pay all entry fees. When a fixed percentage is taken out of this to give to the owner, there is precious little to live on. We chewed the matter over and went to sleep having agreed, 'Let's see what time brings.'

Well, time brought something rather faster than we had anticipated in the form of a loud knocking on the door at around six-thirty in the morning. I staggered out of bed, went downstairs to open the door to a complete stranger.

'What can I do for you?' I asked.

'I've come for O'Malley,' was the reply. A man of decision is Mr Hanson.

Irene showed the natural wifely reaction of some displeasure at the early awakening but it soon became obvious that there was no point in remonstrating with a man who was only doing his job. A nice cup of tea then warmed up our unexpected visitor while I went to the stables, fed the horse, changed his rug, put his halter on and then loaded him into the trailer. And that, so I thought as I watched him being driven away, is the end of O'Malley so far as I am concerned. Not the easiest of rides, not always the straightest or most honest of horses, inclined to be headstrong

– but a horse bang-full of courage and brilliant if you could get the best out of him.

In spite of his setbacks in 1964 his winnings at home had been within £2 of £2900, which, added to the £3745 he had won the year before, meant that Mr Hanson had not done badly. Yet I would be the last one to blame a shrewd Yorkshire businessman, as Mr Hanson undoubtedly was, for trying to do even better. But this turned out to be one of those rare occasions when a decision of his backfired. I'm not sure whether he misread my character and believed I do not always mean what I say or whether he thought it would be a good thing for the horse to have a change of rider. Anyway, I lost the horse and I was not the only loser.

David Barker had always said to me what a great horse O'Malley was and how he had more ability than Mister Softee and I had disputed this. He used to laugh when I told him: 'The boot is on the other foot. Softee is a great and genuine horse.'

Well, David had a chance to test his theory for it was to him that Mr Hanson sent O'Malley after he left me. The new partnership's form in 1965 and 1966 was not spectacular. Apart from winning place money in three competitions, O'Malley did not win a prize of more than £25 in England and failed to win a single class throughout the season except for three equal firsts in preliminaries. He did not even qualify for the Leading Show Jumper of the Year at Wembley, failing to reach earnings of £300.

Eventually, at the end of the season, David and Mr Hanson mutually agreed to end the arrangement and O'Malley was taken over by Alison Westwood, in my opinion one of the best British riders to have emerged since the war. But the horse still was not performing with his old zest, and when we had seen him at White City in July 1966, George Thackray and I both discussed his lack of form with Mr Hanson.

George, I knew, was willing to be part-owner in the horse and I went so far as to make an offer for him. Mr Hanson pondered the suggestion for a while and then

Top left   Although none of my family rode, it was not long before I was on my first pony. This was the first photograph ever taken of me on horseback.

Top right   The look is there, if not the style! This was one of my first public competitions at Bingley Show on a pony called Simon, who earned his keep between gymkhanas by delivering the milk.

Below   Farmer's Boy at Dublin 1958, my first international show outside England.

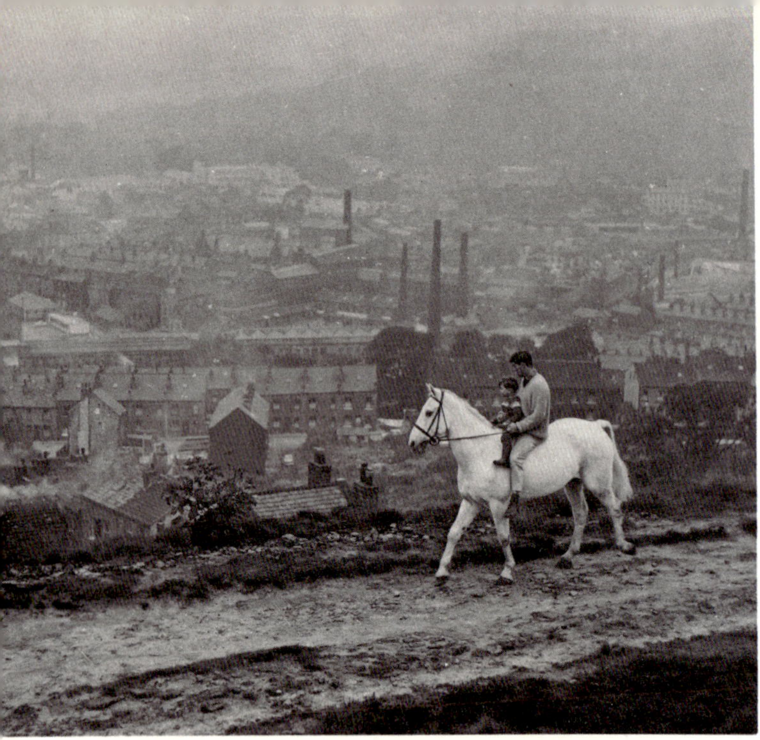

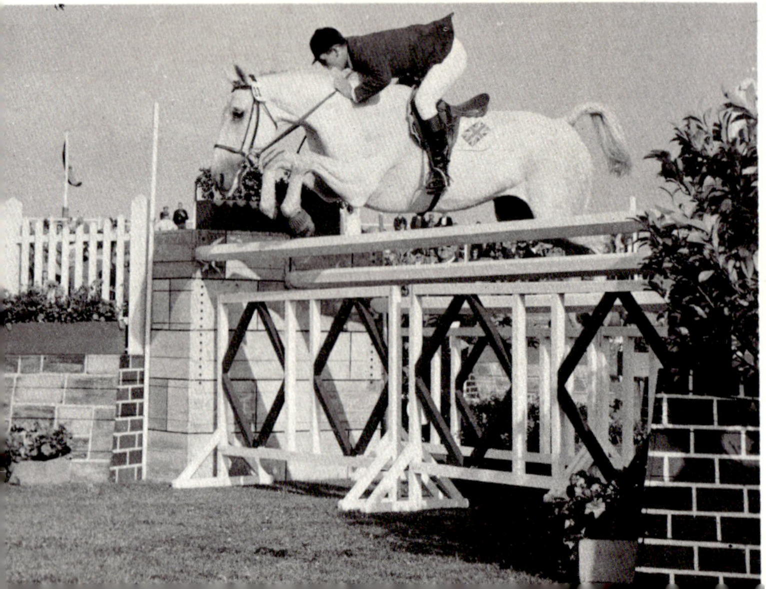

Opposite page   No horse of mine is wrapped up in cotton wool. The two pictures show Warpaint at work and play.

Left   Competing at Aachen in 1964 and *above left* exercising on Gilstead Moor, overlooking Bingley, with Stephen coming along for the ride.

Above right   O'Malley clears a 7 foot wall in the puissance at Toronto. He later cleared 7 foot 3 to win the competition.

Hickstead—coming down the Bank and (*below*) the gesture that launched a thousand quips. My V for Victory sign after Mattie Brown had won the Hickstead Derby has, I think, been the cause of more sporting jokes than anything else I've done. A small selection of the many cartoons following the incident is shown opposite.

Opposite page:
Above Keith Waite of the Daily Mirror.
Centre Rigby of The Sun.
Below Giles of the Daily Express.

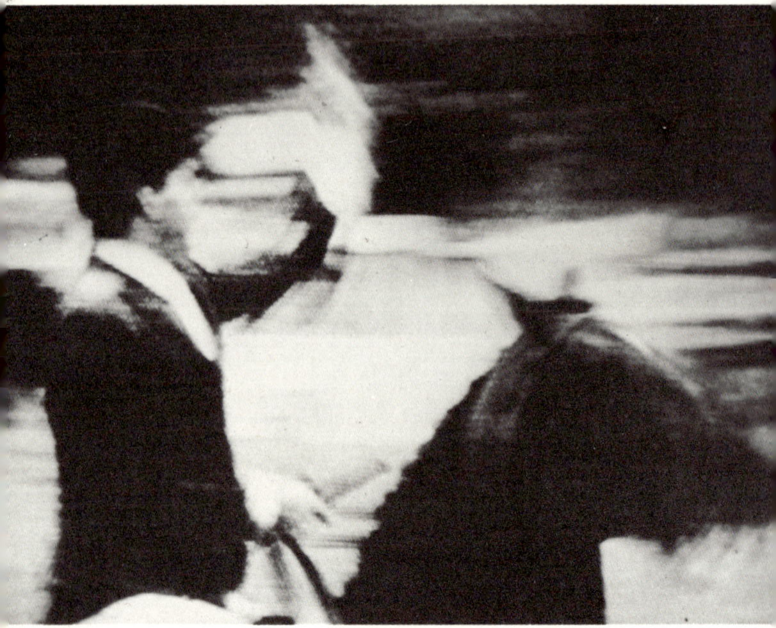

"Isn't he cute—he learnt it from Harvey Smith"

"Ein, zwei, UP! Nein, ve haf to be quicker to beat the Englander Schmidt!"

"Will the comedian who put this here kindly remove it. Mr. Harvey Smith will not be lunching today."

I went into wrestling as a change from show-jumping and as an evening's activity to help me relax. Before long I was competing and now it's not unusual for me to wrestle three nights a week. *Right* Relaxation – the Harvey Smith method !

Above All 25 stone of 'Big Daddy' Crabtree go flying through the air in one of my early competitions.

WRESTLING
FLYING SCOTS
HAMPION MIKE
MARINO
GIANT ZULU WARRIOR
PRINCE KUMALI
BIG JOCK
CAMERON
EDDIE FLASH
HAMMILL
RESTLING
THE SAINTS
UNDERTAKERS
MIGHTY YANKEE
JEFF KAYE
STRONGMAN
ADRIAN STREET
ADRIAN
STREET

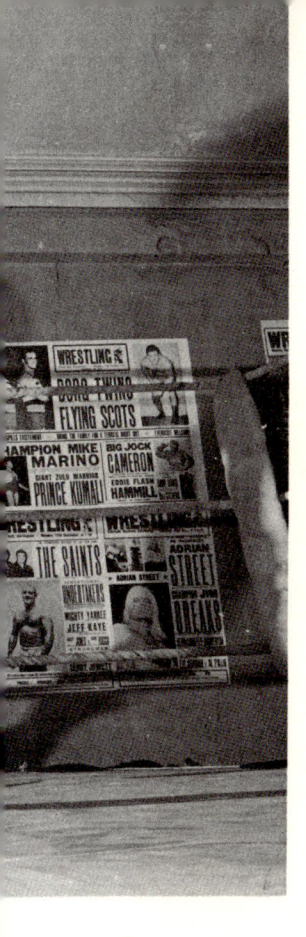

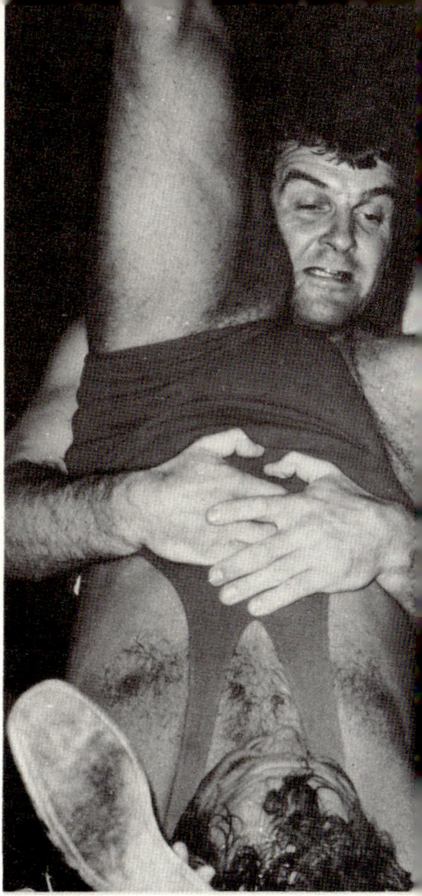

Continuing the family tradition.
Above Irene and I checking the saddle on Stephen's pony.

Left Graham Fletcher, Paddy McMahon and myself enjoying an informal moment at The Horse of the Year Show 1975.

agreed to let me have O'Malley back again. He, in fact, retained the ownership and from that date we resumed the association which had worked so well in 1963 and 1964. Neither of us bore any grudge about the intervening period, and really there was no reason why we should.

While Mr Hanson and I could start again where we left off, O'Malley and I could not. He looked poor, and sorry for himself, and he was lame in front. I drove him from the White City to Mr Hanson's country home at Markham Moor, near Tuxford, and from there Mr Hanson arranged for him to be taken up to Bert Cleminson's place to have his legs put right.

When I got up on him shortly afterwards I found his mouth had gone and that I could not ride him with the accuracy I used to; he was fighting all the time to get away. I had been able to get some purchase on his mouth and keep him happy, but that was not possible any more. I like to keep my horses settled, balanced and relaxed. There is not much distance between some of the fences and it is impossible to get the results when a horse is tearing away at you, as O'Malley did then. What had gone wrong I am not sure for both David and Alison are among the leading British riders. Maybe bits had been tried which were not the ones to work on him, maybe the difference in style and method had been responsible. Still, what did matter to me was that I had to get the old horse going once more and as he had retained both his courage and his big jump I was confident that he would be a good horse again one day.

7. The road to Madrid

My own 1965 season was heralded by big news: the introduction of a new world championship open to nations throughout the world, points being awarded according to placings in the Nations Cup, a maximum of six to count. The championship was given the name of the President's Cup.

The BSJA International Selection Committee planned to send teams to Nice and to Rome, but these outings were cancelled because of a coughing epidemic, and the first foreign trip was to Madrid for the eight-day show beginning on 23 May. The British were out in force, seven riders being chosen with a total of nine horses, John Kidd and myself having two apiece. Irene came with me, getting a welcome break from housework and the job of bringing up Robert and Stephen, our two lads, and we both found Madrid to be the most enjoyable and interesting place we have seen.

The show was held in the grounds of the Club de Campo, an exclusive club with a subscription that eliminated all but the well lined. The setting was just about perfect and our Spanish hosts were very good to us. As with most Continental shows, time had little meaning and often the horses were kept hanging around for a while waiting their turn. There was plenty of shade, though, and the delays did not upset them.

All the British team got on well together and we had great fun from start to finish. The jumping sessions did not begin until well after lunch and as the weather was very hot there was lots of time for sunbathing and swimming. With everything so relaxing, there was a good bit of larking about and, of course, Fred Welch and myself did our share of it.

Like most Englishmen on their first visit to Spain I went to the bull ring to see for myself what bullfighting was like. Freddie Welch and Johnny Kidd came along too, and so did Irene, only we had ringside seats and Irene, who is anti-bloodsports of all kinds, sat by herself in the gods.

I may have got it all wrong and be doing an injustice to the 'sport', but from what I saw and from what I was told by people who know their bullfighting what happens seems to be as follows: the bull comes into the ring and then the picadors enter, mounted on horses which have padded mattress-like protection on their sides. The idea is to let the bull have a go at the horses' sides while the riders use lances to break the muscles at the back of the bull's neck so making sure that the bull cannot lift his head sharply when it comes to the matador's turn. After the bull has been in there ten minutes or so and had a do with the picadors he just does not want to know; they torment him but he does not want to bother. By then it is fairly easy work for the matador.

If the matador was in the ring with the bull from the word go then it would be okay. But enraging the bull before the matador enters is downright cruel and does not make it a contest at all. The horses, incidentally, were petrified when the bull had a go at them and I saw one throw himself down. When the fights were over we had a nose round and found that horses were badly fed. This may be done on purpose: if they were fit and well they would scarper off out of the way. They were also badly marked.

During the show Irene and I were introduced to Count Toptani, author of that one book I read on show-jumping when first coming into the sport, and he invited us back to his penthouse not far from the Club de Campo. He was a thoroughly entertaining man and with the exception of a chat about his saddles, in which I was very interested, I do not think we mentioned horses at all. He had a very impressive library which caught Irene's eye and when the Count noticed her browsing along the rows of books he said he would give her one that would be of benefit to her; he then selected one on mythology. That, he said, was appropriate reading for a young woman.

Let it not be thought that the sunbathing, the swimming, the fun and games and the pleasant social side in any way lessened the team's determination to do well. Far from it; it is not a good thing to have nothing but the jumping to think about for a long show like Madrid.

Our Nations Cup team consisted of Firecrest, Vibart, Freddie's veteran Brule Tout, and Harvester. Opposing us were German, Italian, Portuguese and Spanish teams. The home side had won six of the ten individual classes and the huge and excited crowd were all ready to cheer their men on to a final triumph. It did not come, though, because they lost a bit of form whereas our horses went better than before.

We went last of the teams, Harvester leading off with four faults, and both Vibart and Firecrest matching this to give us twelve faults, four fewer than Portugal and eight fewer than Germany. Harvester was clear next time, Vibart had four, and Brule Tout eight which gave us a maximum of twenty-four. Firecrest was not required to jump a second time because the nearest possible score to ours was the thirty-six of the Germans. Kif-Kif joined Harvester as the only horse to go clear in the second round and brought Spain into third place well ahead of Portugal. The Italians had a disastrous time finishing with 103¼ faults. Harvester had gone like a bomb in this, his Nations Cup début, and it was a good team win, because the Germans had a strong side out – as they always have.

Back in England, when Irene and I made our annual journey down to the White City, I left War Paint and Rolling Hills at home, and jumped Sea Hawk and Harvester, but it was not until the Friday that I got my first win of the show, through Harvester. He chose the £1050 John Player Trophy, the Victor Ludorum, to produce his best performance, so it can be said he chose rightly.

The week after White City, Harvester won the BSJA

North of England Championship at the Royal Lancashire Show, although if I had had another horse to put in I think I would have rested him in preparation for Dublin. Both he and Sea Hawk had been on the road since April and the travelling was beginning to tell on them. Consequently, at Dublin the polish had gone from Harvester and though he was thereabouts he did not get the results he would have done as a fresher horse.

Some importance was attached to the Nations Cup competition there, for the Aga Khan Trophy, as we could not afford to let the Italians pull further ahead in the race for the President's Cup. They fielded the same team as at the White City – The Rock, Canio, Rahin and Ballyblack, whereas Stroller and O'Malley replaced Firecrest and Beethoven for us. It was interesting for me to be in the same team as David Barker and O'Malley and to watch them performing in a competition in which we won a surprise victory. O'Malley's eight faults in the first round were discarded, Stroller being clear and both Harvester and Atalanta faulting only at the water, but it was Harvester's score which we were able to drop in the second. Our total of twenty was eight and three-quarters better than Ireland, twelve better than Holland, twenty-three better than Australia and, strangely, twenty-eight better than Italy for which no horse had fewer than twelve faults.

September found me on my way across the sea again, this time to pay a return visit to the Rotterdam International Show. It was pouring down when we all arrived the day before the start of the show, 'we' being Peter Robeson, William Barker, Judy Crago and Charles Stratton, the chef d'équipe. Alison Westwood (now Mrs Dawes) and Althea Roger-Smith (now Mrs Josh Gifford) were already there, having called at Ostend on the journey down from Copenhagen and helped Britain to win the Nations Cup at both those shows. The arena was terribly soggy and it did not greatly upset me to find out that the box containing Harvester, Sea Hawk and William's pair, North Flight and

Little Dan, would miss the first day because of a mix-up at the docks.

Firecrest did not like the conditions and after being retired in his first competition was left in his box for the rest of the show. On the other hand, The Maverick was in terrific form and won one class on each of the first two days, ending up with the Prix du Vainqueur as the most consistent horse of the show. Harvester was second to our old adversary – Nelson Pessoa's Cangaceiro – in the Prix van de Maas on the third day and I pulled him out the same night for the puissance. He was one of eight clear first time in very bad going and then, in the second, hit a glue-like patch of ground as he went to take off at the big parallel bars. The ground held him and though he managed to get himself over the top bar he couldn't get his under-carriage down in time and stumbled over on landing.

Rarely does a fall do my horses any harm – the reverse is usually the case – and Harvester came out the next day and jumped two clear rounds in the Nations Cup. He was the only horse to do so, though The Maverick might well have equalled the achievement had he been needed in the second round, and Apache, ridden by A. Blickenstorfer, had only one quarter of a time fault for Switzerland. With The Maverick and Harvester going clear in the first round and both Spring Fever and North Flight collecting only twelve faults all told we were easy winners from a good German team and, as a result, Britain virtually clinched the first President's Cup, Rotterdam being the sixth Nations Cup victory of the season for us.

I had left War Paint behind after a good August in which he had won four important classes, including the British Timken Open, and on my return from Rotterdam he promptly came out best in the Cock o' the North at Burghley. After that I travelled down to Hickstead and put him in his last Hickstead Derby. He was going great guns until we came to the bank, which he fell off rather than came down, hitting the bottom hard. His knees buckled from under him and he landed bang wallop, straight on his head. He was shaken but I steadied him up, got on his back and off we went. The fall was his only error.

Next year I entered him for the Derby again and when he got to the top of the bank, he remembered all about his fall and showed no interest in going down again. I thought to myself: 'Well, maybe you are right. If you don't want to go down I am not going to make you,' and I brought him off. There is no point in frightening a horse by compelling him to do something for which you would only be sorry afterwards.

At Wembley's Horse of the Year Show, War Paint was equal first in a preliminary section of the Leading Jumper of the Year and Harvester was among eleven others who joined him over one of Colonel Jack Talbot-Ponsonby's tough and controversial courses in the final. Half the number, including both mine, survived for a second attempt by virtue of having just one fence down, and when War Paint went in again, last of all, none had done any better second time round. He did, so winning the competition that Farmer's Boy had won when I was beginning my climb six years earlier.

Harvester jumped fairly consistently all week, producing his best in the one that mattered, the *Sunday Times* Cup, a competition confined to the top twelve national horses over the season and international show-winners. Once again, the first jump-off failed to produce a single clear round and seven of us with four faults had to go again. Ted Williams took the Argentinian horse, Carnaval, round without a mistake to lead until Harvester, coming in at the end, equalled his performance in a time five seconds faster. At the end of the show the Harringay Spurs came to me, thanks to Harvester and Sea Hawk.

I spent just over a week at home before asking Irene to pack my things again for another trip to the Continent, for the Amsterdam and Brussels Shows.

Brussels was the end of the season for me. I was invited to go with the British team to Geneva in the middle of November and I gladly took the opportunity as my leading two were still going well enough. Most riders are pleased to get over to the Continent after the British season is over, provided there is a bit of a break after Wembley. If you lay off for too long between one season and the next you can lose a bit of judgement and it takes longer to get your horses striding on again.

The international show at Brussels proved to be a highly satisfactory end to the season for us. By winning the Nations Cup, the British team edged the Germans out to win the much coveted President's Cup. In addition, Sea Hawk jumped one of the best rounds of his life to win the Prix de St Hubert and I also came home with the Prix du Leman.

In the table of top horses in the country, published at the end of the season, Harvester replaced O'Malley as the leader for 1965, Sea Hawk was fifth and, for the third year in succession, War Paint was seventh. Just behind Harvester was North Flight, Bess X was third for David Broome and Stroller was fourth. The list would have had to go a long way beyond the top ten to get O'Malley on it.

In the winter months that brought 1965 into 1966 I spent much of my time down at the offices of the family firm, taking some of the load of administrative work off John's shoulders and keeping abreast of the firm's affairs as a director should. When a year is as busy with show-jumping as was 1965 it seems that I am constantly either at a show or on my way to another, yet I am always bobbing back home. John's duties as managing director kept him tied up, but he was always ready, nevertheless, to help me by driving the horses down to the docks, collecting them from the docks or the airport, or carrying out repairs to one of the wagons.

Before the 1966 season I made a trip down to Crippenden Manor for a sale of Russian horses – and found them going cheap. I bought two or three which I liked and brought them up to Gilstead to join another of their countrymen, Sea Bird, whom I had bought at the previous Wembley. He had been owned by Arthur Snipe, well known as an owner of racehorses as well as show-jumpers, and ridden by Jane

Scott. Jane had done fairly well on him, but by the time I bought him Sea Bird had packed it up with her and would not go at all.

He was, in fact, a strange-tempered horse and it was difficult to get through to him. I would take him out one day and teach him a thing and think: 'Now he's got it,' take him back the next day and he would have forgotten all about it. He did become a very good horse, though, and took some beating when he decided to try.

I rushed Sea Bird a bit to start with and took him over with Sea Hawk and War Paint in March to the Frankfurt International Show, held in the Festhalle, a magnificent indoor place. Ted was in the team again, with Mr F. W. Smith's Relincho and Carnaval, John Kidd took Bali H'ai and Alison had not only The Maverick but also O'Malley. This was the first time I had seen Alison on my old horse and he seemed to go quite well for her, jumping one particularly good clear round. Sea Bird did well enough for a novice without setting the Festhalle alight and it was Sea Hawk who got the only win for the British team, scoring in a speed class.

From Frankfurt, the team made their way to Paris for first of the season's Nations Cups.

I had to wait for a few hours after our arrival in Paris to see what the town was like, as we did not get to the stables at the Porte de Versailles until well after midnight. The stables were under the same roof as the main ring and all of us were pleased by the facilities at the show and at the first-rate hotel at which we stayed, close by the Arc de Triomphe. Gerald Barnes was chef d'équipe and this was the first time I had been abroad with him. He had, of course, been a BSJA official for many years, and had seen his daughters win countless classes.

The show rules said I could start only two horses and so I dropped Sea Bird. Ted suffered a blow when Carnaval trod on a nail at the very start of the show and went lame. We got together and between us improvised with a kettle, a tube and a bucket, the purpose being to keep Carnaval

standing in constantly warm water. The kettle we kept on a
Calor gas stove, the tube we ran down to the bucket, and
by replenishing the kettle and emptying the surplus water
in the bucket we kept the temperature of the water just
right. We persevered for three days and eventually it did
the trick, so that Carnaval was fit for the Nations Cup.
Not only was he fit, he was brilliant, being the only horse
in the six teams to jump two clear rounds.

With Pierre Jonqueres d'Oriola, the Olympic champion,
Guy Lefrant, Captain de Fombelle and Charles Dupuy
going well for France, Tony Ebben being in form for
Holland, and the German and Spanish teams getting well
there in the placings, it was obvious that it was going to be
a close Nations Cup. Alison rode O'Malley in it in preference to The Maverick who was out of sorts, and with
Calando lame, George had no option but to ride Brandy
Soda, just as it had to be War Paint for me. Carnaval,
apparently all right again, made up the team.

I led off for us and War Paint jumped one of his really
class rounds. This straight away put pressure on the other
teams, which was increased when Carnaval went clear,
with just one and a quarter time faults. They began to fall
behind us and a four and three-quarter fault score by
Brandy Soda put us clearly in the lead at the end of the
first round. O'Malley improved on his first effort in the
second round, having only one fence down, War Paint
had one down and half a time fault and Carnaval sewed
it up for us by repeating his clear, though with two and a
half time faults. There was no need for George to go in
again. France was second, Spain third and the Germans
only fourth. Italy, not the force she once was, came fifth
with Holland a distant sixth, having no one to give strong
support to Tony Ebben.

Paris was the last of the Continental shows for any
British rider until the back-end of 1966. On 15 May the
Ministry of Agriculture placed a ban on the importation
of horses from Europe, because of an outbreak of swamp
fever over there. This meant that we could not go over to

the Continent ourselves with horses because we would not have been allowed to bring them back until the outbreak was at an end and the statutory clearance period had passed.

At home, I missed the Warwickshire Equestrian Club Show, for a change and began the season at Hickstead, taking Sea Bird, Sea Vixen, my black home-bred filly, and Altar Rock. They dominated the novice classes and for good measure I popped Sea Bird in an Open Gamblers competition. The course included a 5 feet 3 inches gate and he jumped it seven times, backwards and forwards. By the end of the show Sea Bird was Grade A.

Altar Rock was a very good horse and I am sure he would have made the top. I bought him as an unmade three-year-old from Terry Wharton, a York dealer, and he was only four when I took him down to Hickstead. After doing well there I took him to Windsor, where he won the Grade B and the overall championship, then to the Suffolk County, where he was second to Ted Williams's Relincho in the Eastern Counties Open Championship, and shortly after that he won the Open at Holme-on-Spalding Moor. Other that Harvester and Madison Time he was the best novice I have ever had, quick and neat, and a horse who was not going to hit any fences if he could help it.

As a rule I do not have the time which must be devoted to novices, but Altar Rock was worth the extra effort. Things in general were going very well for me. Sea Hawk had come with a bang at Hickstead, winning four classes, and War Paint had won both big classes at Newark. Then came the blow.

The Tuesday after Altar Rock's Open win, Doreen came down to the house – around seven-thirty it would be – and told me that she thought the horse had colic. I went up to have a look at him and found him leaning against the wall and almost toppling out through the stable door. A closer look showed us that it was not colic but that he was para-lysed down one side. Afraid that he would fall through the doorway, I decided to push him along the wall and round the corner of the box so that he would have strong support. I got between him and the wall to shove him along and was doing quite well when, just as I got him round the corner, his back-end swung inwards and crushed me sideways on to the wall. He was a big heavy horse and the force with which he hit me broke my shoulder. Altar Rock slipped to the floor and could not get up. We called the vet and then worked a loose door under the horse and dragged him out into the open.

We laid him down in the paddock beside a wagon and erected a tarpaulin over him – he was too big, at 18 hands, for us to be able to tend him in the box. There he stayed with Doreen by his side day and night, working like a slave to keep him alive. The vet, a local man, worked tremendously hard, too. Doreen and I turned him over every six hours and after six days we got him up for an hour and a half and we really thought we were winning. But when I took a look at him around four o'clock the next morning I found that he was blowing in his lungs. The vet confirmed that he had congestion of the lungs and so the struggle was over; Altar Rock had to be put down. What had caused the paralysis I do not know. He may have been fast on the floor of his box and knocked his head, damaging his brain. But whatever the cause, it was a shame to lose so good a horse in those circumstances.

The legacy for me, of course, was a damaged shoulder. I was advised to stop riding altogether until the break had knitted properly but I could not take that advice with the season just coming to its peak. Instead, I used a stirrup leather to bind the arm nearest to the break against my side. This was working well and the injury was healing nicely when Sea Bird fell with me at the Royal Highland Show and smashed it up again. So it went on. Every time, the bone started knitting together, bang, I would give it another belt. Sea Bird fell again with me at Liverpool, three days before the White City, making things as bad as ever, and the annoying part of it was that both falls were the result of silly little mistakes over easy fences. After a while I started to wear a special strap round my neck to keep my shoulders back and at the same time allow free use of both my arms, and I was still wearing this at the tail end of the season.

Just before the Altar Rock incident, Harvester joined me from Rawcliffe Manor, Bert Cleminson's home. It had looked for a time as though my partnership with Harvester might be at an end for Bert had told me that he was thinking of letting the horse go to his son, Ben, a rider just out of junior classes. Anyway, these plans were changed and Harvester came to me just in time to take him down to the Richmond Royal. Had he got off to a prompt start he would have been first, not third, in the season's Top Ten. At Richmond he warmed up with sixth place in the Simpson Championship and the next day he landed the International Harvester Championship. The limited help I could give him did not prevent him winning the Royal Highland Stakes, the international trial at the Royal Norfolk, the £100 Kenning Trophy at the Sheffield and Hallamshire, and the Walwyn Championship in quick succession after that.

June and July that year were hectic by any standards, In addition to all the horse matters, Irene and I – Irene in particular – had our work cut out moving from our semi in Gilstead Drive into Craiglands Farm, two or three miles further up the road and right on the top of Ilkley Moor. I had known the place as a young lad when it was a poultry farm and when I used to play there with a schoolmate. Later it became a pig enterprise and when we moved in I had to start the job of getting the long single-building piggery made into a series of loose boxes on either side of a central aisle. The farm had about thirty acres of grassland and the house itself, we decided, needed a good bit of modernization. Later, in 1968, I put up a large indoor school which has helped me enormously in the schooling of my horses. The farm's isolated position means that, at home at least, we are out of the public eye.

The 1966 Royal International at the White City took place in July and, for the first time, began on a Sunday. As there were no Continental competitors taking part because of the swamp fever ban, the show fell a bit flat. I ended up with the Loriner's Cup and the Saddle of Honour, but of far more importance to me was the conversation I had with Mr Hanson about O'Malley which led to the old horse coming back to me.

Bert Cleminson is an expert at getting animals sound. and O'Malley was taken from Mr Hanson's country residence to Rawcliffe Manor. Bert had him right in no time. After that I did a bit of work with O'Malley at home and found him low in morale and physical condition.

To me, he seemed short of damned good food and I set about putting that right – and his mouth. His first show with me in 1966 was Shrewsbury, in the middle of August, and he got third in the Grade A. I did another ten or so shows with him after that, just teaching him to jump clean again, something he seemed to have forgotten how to do. I was content to spend the rest of the season re-educating him and keeping him jumping. There would be time enough in the years to come to go after the big stuff.

Fortunately the swamp fever scare ended in time for Marion Coakes (now Mrs Mould), Alison Westwood (Mrs Dawes), Ted Williams and myself to cross over to the Continent for the Brussels and Amsterdam International Jumping Shows. Brussels began the week after Wembley and all our horses did fairly well, Stroller in particular.

As I made my way back to Craiglands I knew I would have plenty to do in the months before show-jumping started again. There were the novices to school, farm alterations to plan, my duties as a director to attend to and plenty of jobs around the house to tackle.

It was and is a full life.

8. The clock that stopped

What 1966 lacked in incident 1967 certainly made up for.

There was, for instance, my dispute with the British Show Jumping Association which had its origins at the Wilmslow (Cheshire) Show and which left a bad taste in my mouth. It all started with a sponsored class in which I jumped my new German horse, Silver Knight. He was one of six to go forward to the final jump-off and was drawn first.

He jumped what I knew was a topping round and when he came out of the ring I felt sure under my hat that his time wasn't going to be beaten. When the next horse, North Flight, was a second slower I knew the job was over because William Barker's mare was a very, very good horse against the clock. Later on, in came Vibart and he didn't go fast at all. Speed, in any case, was the least of his virtues and even when he did try to go like hell against my horses he would be five or six seconds behind within a minute.

When Vibart was halfway round on this particular occasion I noticed that the electric clock had stopped at twenty-two seconds. Vibart went on jumping well, but not fast enough, and there was a prolonged silence from the judges' box after he had gone through the finish. The pause ended with the announcement of a time for Vibart which was one and a half seconds better than Silver King's and he was given out as the winner.

I was astonished. My immediate reaction was to jump over the fence round the box, shoot up the stairs, push the door open and ask them straight out: 'How did you get that result?' It was explained to me that when the timing failure occurred the official on the clock saw it and called to the judge: 'The clock has stopped.' The judge then felt for the stop-watch on his wrist and clicked it on. Then, from a distance of some fifty yards directly in front of the finish he had to try to assess exactly when Vibart crossed the line and press the watch again. Anyone who has ever used a stop-watch will realize that human reactions being what they are the judge could not possibly have started his watch within two seconds of the timing device's going wrong, and it was impossible for him to see precisely when Vibart crossed the finishing line. To do that he would have had to be bang in line with the two markers.

'How much time have you allowed for the delay between the clock's stopping and you getting your watch going?' I asked the judge. 'Oh, I haven't allowed any,' he replied. 'Anyway, I can't do much about it now and the result must stand.'

It was a ridiculous situation and I put my feelings into words: 'Judged like that, it's a bloody fiddle,' I told them.

The officials at first didn't show any inclination to think again but I wouldn't wear it and kept at them. Eventually, they suggested as a compromise that they should make Vibart and Silver King equal first and split the prize money. 'Fair enough, I'm quite satisfied at that,' I commented. Andrew Fielder, Vibart's rider, seemed satisfied, too, and as far as I was concerned that was the end of the incident. I appreciated that the officials had been caught on the hop and that they were not trying to show favour to anyone in particular. That is why I was content to share the prize when I knew that it should have been mine outright.

When I left Wilmslow that same night there was no sign that the officials had any misgivings and the whole affair went clean out of my mind. Things, however, were happening behind the scenes over the next few days and about a fortnight later I received notification to attend an enquiry into the incident. I was instructed to appear before the BSJA Disciplinary Authority in London, accused of unseemly behaviour towards a show official. A similar charge brought against Mr Michael Kane, the Renfrewshire farmer and show-jumping enthusiast, had recently resulted in his being suspended for a year.

I hadn't much confidence in the BSJA procedure and with Mr Kane's punishment in mind I was not happy about my prospects. As it was I could not get to London on the appointed day because I had to attend a board meeting of the firm at the quarry and the hearing was switched to a later day at Manchester. I know, of course, that someone had been out to make trouble. There's no shortage of people who want to pull you down when you are at the top; they can't beat you in the ring so are always trying to beat you out of it.

Given the opportunity, I would have been legally represented at the hearing. The BSJA rule referring to its conduct and powers, though, stated: 'No member shall be entitled to be represented when appearing before any of the Disciplinary Authorities.' And it added that any member guilty of unseemly conduct in the opinion of the stewards of the Association could, among other things, be fined a sum not exceeding £100 or suspended for a period not exceeding twelve months. So I was on my Jack Jones when I went in to meet the stewards. For once, though, I was very glad to see the press out in force. I reasoned that if the stewards did come to a really bad decision they would get themselves into trouble.

If the stewards were fair, then I knew that the severe penalties would not apply and I would really have fancied my chances in open court. My case was that I was referring to the method by which the result of the Wilmslow competition had been arrived at when I said it was a fiddle. And in the north we don't take exception to the word 'bloody'. If I were to call someone a bloody fool, he would have every right to object to being called a fool; the adjective is neither here nor there.

As the enquiry warmed up I quickly sensed that whereas one steward was quite willing to try to see my side of the business, there was one other seemingly intent on teaching me a lesson. The two Wilmslow officials were there and, I thought, gave an accurate picture of the whole affair, admitting what they had admitted to me in the box at the show – that no time was allowed for the lapse of time between the clock's stopping and the starting of the stop-watch.

I was able to call several witnesses who were able to testify that they agreed with me about the relative speeds of Silver King and Vibart so that eventually it all boiled down to the fact that I had used a swear word in the judges' box. My handicap was that none of my witnesses had been up in the box with me and there was no one to back me up in my assertion that the 'bloody' had not been aimed at the judge. So I was found guilty of unseemly conduct and fined £50. It didn't matter that the enquiry had confirmed the original reason for the protest, that later the BSJA introduced a new rule which makes it compulsory where electric timing is in use that a stop-watch should also be used as a safeguard, so that a similar error cannot happen again.

My relations with the BSJA have never been too smooth and many is the time when my criticism of the Association has ruffled a few feathers within the show-jumping establishment. Its trouble, I think, is that it has always been much of a military set-up. It tends to be run by people who have retired from the Services, and several of them, it seems to me, find it difficult to forget that they are no longer part of an army unit.

They have a problem, admittedly, because the judges, stewards and other officials at the shows are volunteers and if they are made to look silly some may take their bats home, but the BSJA should not allow this consideration to sway their judgement and repeatedly make the competitor the scapegoat. The idea that they should try to sort things out with competitors and work with them rather than against them does not seem to have crossed the minds of some of the men in power. They believe they have the upper hand and can dictate their terms all the time.

To direct things and see that the hard work gets done there must be one strong man at the top, determined yet sympathetic to the needs of the competitors. This is not the case in the BSJA. If you are working for one boss you know what he wants and can please him: if you are working for half a dozen you cannot please them all.

The BSJA attitude tends to encourage all the 'good sports' who do as they are told without question, whether or not what they are told is right or wrong. But this type of competitor has not got the right stuff in him and is not going to get the results that British show-jumping needs at international level. Some of them if told to go to the North Pole and stand on their heads would set off straight away.

If you stand up for what you think is right it does not endear you to certain officials. Mix in a good deal of success with your outspokenness and you can sit back and wait for the sniping to begin. Generally it has to be ignored even though it can be annoying; and on rare occasions it can give you a bit of fun.

This was the case at a big show in a very wet, blowy day. There was a big class on and I saddled up Harvester about fifteen minutes before he was due to go in. I was just walking him to the collecting ring when I saw this little man bobbing between the tents, peeping at me.

'Right, my lad,' I thought to myself, 'I know your game, and I'll give you something to go on with.' So I began to look furtively around me as though I was making sure that I was not being watched. Then I took Harvester away from the main ring and down towards a quiet corner of the showground, going just slowly enough for my little spy to keep up. Occasionally I caught a glimpse of him, growing increasingly red but with a look of excitement in his eyes, as he dashed along behind the tents and hedges. When I got to the quiet corner there was this little figure ready and waiting for his moment of glory; for he was going to be the man to catch Harvey Smith 'rapping' his great horse, Harvester. He'd had to cover more than half a mile but he had stuck to his task and, by golly, he was going to be well in with the BSJA when he reported all the dreadful facts. I couldn't see his face when I did just one circle on Harvester and cantered back to the collecting ring, but I would have liked to.

The 1967 jumping season began earlier than ever for me, in mid-February, at s'Hertongenbosch, in Holland, at a new show held in the cattle market there. It drew good crowds and all the top Continental riders, and the organization matched the high standard of the jumping. I felt sure it would become a really good show, and it has. I took War Paint, Sea Hawk and Harvester over and as I had not even sat on the backs of the greys since the year before, they needed the classes at s'Hertongenbosch to get going.

I travelled over with Doreen, having made my entries on a purely individual basis, and found that Marion Coakes and her father, Ralph, as well as Ann Townsend were making tours, too. Ann stayed on for Dortmund and Hanover and Marion and I also went on to Frankfurt and Antwerp. The Westphalle Hall at Dortmund is one of the finest indoor set-ups in the world. It serves several purposes, there being a cycle track round the outside of the ring, and as an indoor jumping centre it is just about perfect. The arena itself is very big for an indoor one, the stables and exercise ring are under the same roof as the arena and, as always with the Germans, everything runs efficiently and punctually.

While I was at Dortmund I took a liking to a horse called Silver King who I could see was too strong a horse for his very useful rider, Hauke Schmidt, and I kept on at Hauke about buying him. There seemed to be nothing doing in that direction until, talking together in our hotel around midnight, Hauke had a change of mind. There and then we decided to go down to the stables and get Silver King out for me to have a try on him. This I did, and I promptly bought the horse for a Lincolnshire owner, Mr J. E. Taylor. Hauke took Silver King home after Dortmund and then drove him to Antwerp for me and I took charge of him there. I thought he was a big, genuine and bold horse, and he proved this in his few months with me.

My trio were just finding their form by the time I moved on to Hanover where Harvester won the Grand Prix from a little horse called Fairness, who broke down trying to beat him.

From Hanover it was on to Frankfurt where things went better for the small English group, Harvester and Sea Hawk both winning on the opening day and Stroller on the next. There was a long gap between Frankfurt and the last show on this pre-season indoor circuit, Antwerp, where, as arranged, I picked up Silver King in readiness to travel him back with my other horses. Harvester again went well and won a have-a-gamble competition on the second day and Sea Hawk, too, did reasonably.

War Paint's last international show was not his most successful though, as always, he did his best. He was being overshadowed by my others and I decided to lease him out for the home season. He still had plenty of ability if unable to match such as Harvester and O'Malley, and I knew he would do well enough.

With War Paint's departure for a stable up Durham way I was left with Harvester, O'Malley, Sea Bird, who by this time had become Fen Bird (something to do with the Fen country, perhaps), Sea Hawk and Silver King, as well as one or two youngsters, including Sea Vixen. Antwerp ended on 20 March and that gave me only a short spell at home before taking off for Nice, the official French international show of the season. I left Silver King and Harvester behind while I went to Nice, taking instead O'Malley and Fen Bird. One of them travelled in Douglas Bunn's wagon and the other in Alison Westwood's, all the riders flying out.

Douglas was chef d'équipe and combined those duties with riding Beethoven, Alison took just The Maverick, Anneli Durmmond-Hay's Merely-a-Monarch was accompanied by a new horse called Frenchman and Peter Robeson had his pair, Firecrest and Joycott. Both the horses and ourselves were well satisfied with our accommodation. We riders were in a sea-front hotel a short drive from the Palais des Expositions – the site for the show – and the stabling was on the magnificent Nice racecourse. The boxes were actually in the centre of a whole series of racetracks: flat, hurdle and steeplechase, and there was another with a different surface for the trotters. Ascot is a pup at the side of

Nice. The people who want, and can afford, to follow racing down there are very lucky.

To make things just about perfect for us the sun hardly ever stopped shining and as there was only one jumping session a day starting at around eight p.m., we had all the swimming and sunbathing we could wish for. As was to be expected at a place like Nice, the social side fairly buzzed and at one of the cocktail parties to which the team was invited there were enough big names to keep the class-conscious happy for months. The Duke of Edinburgh was there, and accompanying him were Princess Anne and Prince Charles, while Princess Grace of Monaco represented the local royalty. Elizabeth Taylor and Richard Burton were among the guests as well.

Early in the show the water caused a lot of trouble to the British horses yet by the end of the first week all were jumping it well enough. Merely-a-Monarch and The Maverick did best of our horses during the first three days, though The Maverick was left out of the Nations Cup line-up on the Thursday, the sixth jumping day. O'Malley went first of the twenty horses and collected four faults at the water, but these were discarded when Monarch, Beethoven and Firecrest all jumped clear. The French, fielding three of their Tokyo silver medallists, also had a blank score and Brazil had only four and three-quarter faults. Italy, without the d'Inzeos, could do no better than twelve faults and an inexperienced German team was lying a poor last of five. O'Malley had a decent clear second time, Monarch and Beethoven both followed suit and it was not necessary for Firecrest to go again: you cannot do better than that.

The second rest day of the show followed and then, on the Saturday, came the Grand Prix. Our horses were bang in form and all five got through the first round safely, The Maverick having been added to the Nations Cup four. Sometimes after a particularly good effort by British horses in a leading competition, like a grand prix, there is a tendency for people to think we have ridden as a team and chefs d'équipe have a habit of saying so. But a grand prix is an individual contest and not a team event and whereas riders will tell any other member of the team whatever that member wants to know, I, for one, do not ride as a team member but for myself. This is standard practice for top internationals.

This time I was first of the eight to go in the jump-off and O'Malley jumped one of his best ones to go clear again in 49.5 seconds, more than three seconds faster than Firecrest, the only other horse not to get a fence down. Merely-a-Monarch was a bit unlucky in that he just got a touch at the water in a faster time than O'Malley, and Beethoven and The Maverick went fast enough to beat the other fourfaulters. So the result read O'Malley first, Firecrest second, Monarch third, Beethoven fourth and The Maverick fifth – as far as I know the first time ever that one nation has had the first five in a grand prix. I was pleased enough with O'Malley, yet the mouthing troubles were still there and, I knew, were going to take a long time to cure.

All told, most of the horses did their bit at Nice and it was a contented bunch of riders who made their way back to England. There was just time for me to say hello to Irene, Robert and Stephen before I set out for the Rome Horse Show, starting on 23 April, five days after the end of Nice. Irene decided it was time for a holiday and booked a charter flight out. She makes the most of her foreign trips, getting around a lot as well as catching up on her reading and watching a bit of the jumping.

O'Malley got into the placings six times at Rome and this consistency brought him the award of Champion Horse of the Show and me the title of Leading Rider. For this I received a cup originally presented to the show by the father of Piero and Raimondo d'Inzeo – and it gave me a good deal of pleasure to receive the cup from Raimondo.

Because of my Continental trips I had done very little jumping in England by that time but a 'Christmas parcel' had kept the horses I had not taken abroad in good trim and three or four days after I got back from Rome I had a happy time at the Royal Windsor. The 'parcel' was, in fact, young William Halliday, the lad who all those years ago had been in the box when it overturned in Scotland. William, born and bred in Bingley, had helped me as a boy and wanted to go with horses when he left school. I would not give him a job until he had served an apprenticeship, and he chose baking. In the meantime, William's family went out to Canada and when William finished serving his time he went out to join them. He had been there about nine months, when he sent Irene and me a Christmas card saying 'Parcel to follow'. Then one day he arrived at the house and when Irene asked him: 'Where's that parcel you promised us?' he admitted that he was it.

'I have just landed, I have no money, nowhere to live and I haven't got a job. How about it?' he asked.

'Okay,' I told him, 'you're a groom.' He had done a bit of riding as a boy and soon picked things up. He was with me on and off for some years, and eventually won several good classes before leaving the sport in 1976.

While I had been in Nice and Rome he had kept Silver King ticking on and at the Royal Windsor in mid-May the German horse did something his former owner had said he would never do – win a speed class. On the Saturday, Sea Hawk won the 'have-a-gamble' and then Harvester won first the Open and then the David Brown Tractors Supreme Championship, having plenty of time to spare in the championship over Stroller and Franco, who was going well for Caroline Bradley.

Wilmslow Show in May had seen the ridiculous mix-up over the timing failure and the BSJA hearing was eventually held in July. That hearing and the treatment I got made me determined to hit them at the White City, and I would have hit them even harder but for a bad decision at the water in the King George V Cup which made me gnash my teeth a bit.

There were four of us in the jump-off: O'Malley, Alan Oliver on Sweep, Peter Robeson and Firecrest, and David Broome and Mister Softee. Sweep collected four faults to drop out before the third round in which I took O'Malley in first. Now, when you are jumping the water you can see when your horse puts his feet out and reaches for it, and when he does this you know he is going to get the distance. On this occasion O'Malley did reach out and he was well clear. Yet the judge disagreed. O'Malley went on to fault at the wall and the double but he would not have done so had I not seen that the flag was up at the water and I believe he would have won. Instead Peter took Firecrest round for first place and Mister Softee edged O'Malley into third.

Other results read like this: *Horse and Hound* Cup – first, O'Malley; Phillips Electrical Stakes – first, Sea Hawk; Moss Bros Puissance Championship – equal first, Goodbye and Harvester, equal third, O'Malley and Charleston; *Country Life* and *Riding* Cup – first, Sea Hawk; GRA Stakes – first, Sea Hawk; John Player Trophy – first, Harvester. The John Player win was Harvester's third on the trot and my fourth in all, O'Malley having won it in 1962. The course for the *Daily Mail* Cup – the Grand Prix – was not big enough to suit Harvester whose clear round in the jump-off was slower than that of Mancinelli's Petter Patter, who hadn't really deserved to win, and the little Polish horse, Drobnica, who certainly did deserve to add the *Daily Mail* to his triumph in the Gamblers Stakes earlier in the week.

The Nations Cup (the Prince of Wales) had only four teams in it and was not exactly a sparkling affair. O'Malley, Havana Royal and Softee gave us a no-fault score in the first round and our second-round total of eight was still below the best first-round score of the others. That was the last Royal International at the White City and I, for one, had no regret about the switch to Wembley. The White City was not the best of places at which to hold an international show: the stables were 300 yards down the road from the stadium and the warm-up area was small and surfaced with cinders. There was always the risk of laming a horse there. The main thing in its favour was the restaurant from which you could watch the jumping and have a decent meal at one and the same time.

9. The dopers get to work

The Royal Lancashire at Blackpool in the first week of August brought to a head a situation which had been nagging at me for more than two years and which had already passed one crisis point.

One noticeable thing about my horses is their consistency: they come out day after day exactly the same. But I had begun to notice over the years that all at once, for no apparent reason, I would get on one of them and it would be like climbing on a dead horse. There would be no life there and when I took the horse down to a fence he would kick it down half a dozen times and think nothing about it.

Blackpool 1967 – the Royal Lancashire – set me thinking about all such occasions and I really started putting two and two together. The incident which sparked this off happened after I had put O'Malley in his box on the eve of the show. Not content with fastening the catch and the bolts, I secured the door with a rope. When Doreen went to his box the following morning it was open and empty, and we eventually found O'Malley in the car-park, his belly full of grass and his legs brayed to pieces as a result of chasing about on the concrete roadways. He was due to jump in one of the big classes on the opening day but had to be pulled out, and although I tried him on the second day he could not get off the ground at all.

I knew O'Malley could not have got out of his box by himself and that someone must have deliberately opened the door. The evidence of a person I know confirmed this. He was walking through the horse line around five-thirty a.m. when he saw a rider well-known to me coming away from O'Malley's box. The rider's employer had been overheard to boast that he could stop me from winning any time he chose to do so. It was easy for him to stop O'Malley at Blackpool. All his rider did was come out on the pretence of giving his horses a school, then the rider slipped into the row of boxes, opened the stable door and – good day. It was his bad luck that the rider was seen and that I should be told that he had been seen.

From the Royal Lancashire I went up to the Durham County where I was about to turn in for the night when I saw my suspect again. There was no reason for him to be there at all, as he did not have a horse entered. There was only one thing to do and that was to mooch about all night and make sure that my horses were not tampered with. The effort was worth it and the next day I got first, second and two other placings in the main event, the Earl of Durham Open. If I had left them unattended for the night the result would have been quite different.

At Southport, later that month, I was at the receiving end again, or rather Sea Hawk was. As soon as I got him out of the box and sat on his back I told Doreen: 'This horse is useless.' I took him in the ring and he had five or six fences down, and this is something Sea Hawk just never did. That was at two o'clock in the afternoon. I put him back in his box until five and then he came out and won a minor class. The big money had been for the one before, and that was no coincidence.

When a horse like Sea Hawk jumps absolutely out of character in one event and then comes out three hours later his old self it means that for some reason or other he was not himself in the first one. It has nothing to do with normal loss of form.

There are a thousand and one ways in which a horse can be 'stopped'. Two of the simplest are to throw in an armful or two of hay or give them a lot of water. I keep my horses a bit short of hay and they get nothing for about four hours before they jump. If someone comes along and chucks some hay to them they are straight into it, stuffing themselves. Just as an athlete could not perform well on top of a big meal, neither can a horse. The result is more certain if, like O'Malley, a horse is turned out of his box and allowed to eat his fill and, in addition, bang his legs up as he careers around in his new-found freedom.

Occasionally more drastic steps are taken to stop a jumper, as they were with War Paint at the Horse of the Year Show in 1966. After plaiting him up in his box before a class Doreen left him for no more than ten minutes to get his saddle and bridle. When she came back she gave a final check to the plaits and as she did so noticed a pin-prick on War Paint's neck. When Doreen pointed it out to me I straight away decided to call in a veterinary surgeon and he gave his firm opinion that the horse had been doped. A blood test was taken on behalf of the BSJA but this was found to be negative. Neither myself nor the vet were satisfied that this proved War Paint hadn't been doped; all it proved was that the dope did not show up in the blood-stream. And the vet was definite that the horse had been injected with a hypodermic syringe.

I could not do anything about it then, as I had not any proof, but the Royal Lancashire the next year changed all that and when I talked things over with Charles Stratton and Captain Webber, of the BSJA, they agreed to have a word with Colonel Ansell. The Colonel decided to have precautions taken at Wembley for the Horse of the Year Show and the combination of a guard dog and the knowledge that security men were on the look-out for them almost frightened my suspects to death. They did not go near the boxes and I had a very good Wembley.

I started to think about what had happened on trips to Wembley even before the War Paint doping. The Horse of the Year Show lives up to its name and is the big show of the season in Britain; when I put my horses into it they go down in tip-top condition, usually bucking and squealing, and fit to win a race. But from time to time over the years, when I had pulled them out of their boxes I had found them sluggish. I had known something was wrong and yet I had not really thought that someone was trying to stop them. Things went wrong only when the horses were stabled at a showground. I have never found the horses going anything but well when I have travelled from home to a show.

I have not had the undivided attention of the nobblers. One day, after I had been talking to David Broome about the way my horses had been got at, David came along and asked me to have a look at Softee. The horse had definitely been hit on his cannon bone with a sharp instrument, possibly a firing iron, the intention perhaps being to pop a splint up.

I was convinced that the culprits had been busy with dope as well as using the more obvious methods. I believed it was my responsibility to see that my horses were safe and I took measures which would make sure that whatever showground they were on, they would not be stopped again. These measures worked.

As soon as the Durham County was over I set off across the sea again, this time the Irish Sea, to Dublin and to the wild social routine which is unique to the show. I got an extra bit of interest this time by being invited by one of the stewards to go flying in his plane and I also did a bit of business, buying a little horse called Peggy's Pride from Paddy Griffin. Tommy Wade told me a bit about the horse early in the week and later I watched him jump a few fences outside the ring. To me everything was A1 about him, although I did not have a try on him. Everyone knew he was for sale and both the Italians and the Swiss were trying him, but he had a reputation for putting in a stop and I was able to pull him from under their noses while they hesitated.

Once again, here was a horse who lacked confidence. He would give every fence three or six inches to spare rather than have a tap. I knew a bit about his history and his breeding. He was a seven-year-old and had been bred by Paddy, by Renwood, sire of Seamus Hayes' great horse, Goodbye. At four he won a point-to-point and later he had a few different riders. The one who rode him in 1967 did not get on with him and the horse had not been doing well when it was decided to send him to Dublin and sell him.

There were troubles for me to get over with him but I knew they would right themseves in time and I believed he could turn out to be one of the best jumpers Britain has seen. Meanwhile, I hurriedly changed his name – I could not stand Peggy's Pride. My choice was Condor and later, after I had given him to Irene, his name was changed to Doncella. Later he became Mattie Brown, winner of successive Hickstead Derbies. With War Paint and Sea Hawk now firmly in the veteran class it was a good time to get a young horse on the way up to join another in the same category whom I had bought the previous month. His name was Harney Peak, a Grade A with good prospects.

O'Malley's equal third in the Grand Prix kept me just ahead of Seamus Hayes for the Ballsbridge Trophy awarded to the leading rider of the show.

Late August saw me off again to the Continent with the British team for the Rotterdam International Horse Show, which included the European Championship. Harney Peak joined O'Malley and Harvester for the trip and turned out to be the only one of the three to be 100 per cent fit, though too inexperienced to achieve much. Harvester's trouble had its origins at home. The lad had been exercising him and after getting off him to open a gate he caught the draw rein as he mounted again. Harvester reared up and put his front legs over a wall, taking the skin off the outside of a knee. At Rotterdam he pulled out stiff on the first two or three days and though he improved as the show went on he was never quite right. O'Malley quickly put himself out of the show by getting in too close to the water, a sunken concrete trough, and cutting the back tendon as he tried to find his own solution to the problem. So, all in all, it was not my best Rotterdam.

The European Championship was decided over four events instead of the usual three, all on separate days. Little Drobnica, the Polish horse, won the first with Jan Kowalczyk and I was only eleventh with a stiff Harvester. David Broome, the other British rider, was reasonably placed with

Mister Softee, being fifth. The second event was supposed to be a puissance but Jan Jurgens built a simple little course and there were seventeen clears, including Mister Softee, Harvester and the title-holder, Nelson Pessoa, on Gran Geste, who had been third in the previous stage. A good Nations Cup type course was set for Event 3, which Gran Geste won from Harvester and Softee and this left Nelson with a nice lead over David, Alwin Schockemohle and myself.

All Nelson needed to do was get in the first three in the last event, though this was no easy task with the cream of Europe's riders in the field. The event was held over two courses, the first of eighteen fences – a third puissance, a third supposedly Nations Cup and the remaining six designed to test manoeuvrability. Softee jumped his very best to go clear in a time nearly seven seconds better than the second horse and this pushed David forward as a real danger to Nelson, especially as Gran Geste kicked two out. Harvester had one fence down in that first round and then in the second, for which the puissance fences were left out, he went clear, as did Softee. Gran Geste did even worse than in the first round and Nelson's title chance had gone. David was the European champion, for the second time, and it was also the second occasion on which Softee had won the championship, David Barker having been on him when he scored in 1962.

Softee at his best – and he was at his best at Rotterdam – was a very good horse and a genuine one, and when the going had some give in it he was always in with a chance, especially over the type of courses he met at this show. He did not find long doubles and big parallels too easy. David was just the rider for him and if I had to be beaten I would as soon it was David as anyone because I have great respect for him as a rider and as a competitor. Harvester, by the way, was fourth in the final phase of the championship and this put me in second overall place, ahead of Alwin, Nelson and the Pole.

The Nations Cup this time took a bit of winning, as we

were opposed by France, Switzerland, Germany, Poland, Russia, Holland, Belgium and Ireland, but Stroller, Firecrest, Softee and Harvester did it comfortably with eight faults to spare over the Germans. In the first leg I had a quarter of a time fault on Harvester, which may need some explaining. He was actually the fastest thing on four legs but I got too careful on him, especially when he was getting tired. Softee ended the show by winning the Grand Prix and making David leading rider.

After Rotterdam I passed a fairly uneventful month before the Horse of the Year Show came round again. It was one of the best Wembleys I have had and both the Wembley and the Harringay Spurs came to me. As usual one or two 'good stories' came out of the show. First, there was the turpentine affair, dealt with later in the chapter, and then Douglas Bunn marched out of the place because of his dissatisfaction with the courses being built by Colonel Jack Talbot-Ponsonby. At first Douglas did not say anything; he just showed what he thought by taking Beethoven home. But when the press pestered him with questions he passed one or two comments which made indignation rise high among the people who matter.

Later Ted Williams, David Broome and I stated in print that we were in support of Douglas. We were not sticking up for his attitude towards the courses but we were backing him all the way in saying what he wanted to say. Every man has a right to an opinion, whether the BSJA rulers think so or not; and if a rider wishes to criticize any aspect of the show or of the Association he must be within his rights. We do not want dictatorship in show-jumping or in anything else.

My first win came on the Wednesday in the Leading Show Jumper of the Year contest for the Ovaltine Championship, for which only horses who have won £300 or more during the year can enter. It was Harvester's third win in the Leading Show Jumper. He hit a couple of fences in beating Pitz Palu, but this was Harvester. When he was going really well he did take a feel at them.

Harvester went lazy on me twice early in the *Sunday Times* Cup and had fences down that he should not have done, so I went lazy on him going into the double so that he would hit it. As soon as he had had a fence down, in fact, I was getting him ready for the Victor Ludorum the night after. But I overdid things and Harvester hit the double far harder than I intended and fell. It was a bad miscalculation on my part and if there is anything I hate it is to have a horse on the floor. It does them no good and it can cause injury. Fortunately, Harvester was not hurt and he took the lesson to heart, trotting in from Royal Searcher in the Ronson Trophy, the Victor Ludorum.

That was the end of my English campaign in 1967. Harvester was top horse, as he had been two years earlier and it meant that one of my horses headed the Top Ten for the fourth year out of five. O'Malley, winner in 1963 and 1964, did not do sufficient shows in Britain to stand much chance in the list this time.

Less than a fortnight after Wembley I set off for the United States as a member of a team which looked strong on paper but, in fact, proved to be 'over the top', at the end of a long season. I had Harvester and O'Malley, Andrew Fielder had Vibart, Marion Coakes Stroller, Peter Robeson Firecrest, Ted Williams – who had done well on the North American circuit ten years earlier – took Relincho and Carnaval, and Caroline Bradley partnered Franco. The horses went ahead of us with the grooms and we flew from London Airport on 21 October.

Things did not look promising when we arrived. Riots caused by anti-Vietnam War agitators were in full swing and National Guardsmen were ringing their Armoury Building, in which the Washington International Show was to be held. We were given strict instructions not to go downtown, a restriction which was of more concern to Irene, who had made the trip with me, than to myself. Irene is very keen to get the maximum interest out of her journeys abroad and before the five-week tour was over she had more than made

D

up for the restricted start. Our American hosts were very friendly and seemed genuinely glad to see us.

A nice touch was the appointment of a Miss Hospitality, sash and all, to act as guide and helper to the British team. Judy, the name behind the sash, really was a great help, and the Miss Hospitality idea is one which might be adopted with profit by other international shows.

After a good night's sleep on the Saturday we met the American and Canadian teams at a luncheon given by Mrs Randolph, Master of the Piedmont Hounds. By this time Colonel Harry Llewellyn, our chef d'équipe, had joined us from up at Expo 67. I have many friends among both rival teams and for Irene and me it was especially good to see Kathy Kusner again.

Kathy is just about the best company in the world and we have had some great fun with her. It was she who got me keen on flying, at Rotterdam in 1965. She saw I was interested in watching the little planes going in and out of the airport there and gave me a book on flying. Kathy was already a qualified pilot. Her enthusiasm was infectious and Peter Robeson, too, started to think seriously about taking it up. Peter's keenness waned but I later booked a course of lessons at Yeadon (Bradford/Leeds) Airport and after thirty hours' flying experience I obtained my pilot's licence.

Since 1956 the American team horses and riders have been under the direct control of Bert (Bertalan) De Nemethy, a Hungarian aristocrat and former cavalry officer. De Nemethy has his finger on them the whole year round and he is so brilliant a trainer, stableman and tactician that he has built his team into one of the finest in the world.

He is fortunate, of course, in that the owners are wealthy and that there is no pressure on their horses to attempt to earn their keep. Consequently, they are always fresh and well for the big occasion. Team members spend anything up to six or seven hours a day in the saddle during the off-season. De Nemethy himself tries out all the horses which owners wish to offer on loan to the team and his daily routine can include riding a dozen or so horses. The facilities at the Gladstone Riding Centre, near New York, are superb and the whole organization is typical of American efficiency at its best.

What Britain could do with a man like De Nemethy! Not that the complete American system would work over here. The economics of jumping are so different that it could not closely follow a similar pattern, and I for one would not dream of letting anyone take my horses away. But without doubt we need one man at the top to supervise our international horses and riders; to be there to help when things go wrong; to study the riders' styles and improve on them but not attempt to change them, and to be the permanent chef d'équipe. In my experience I have met only one man who could have filled the bill – Captain Eddie Goldman, principal of the Cheshire Equestrian Centre. Eddie proved his ability as a trainer by the results his riders achieved in every form of equestrian sport. And he could have been a good chef d'équipe.

In view of the fact that our horses were beyond their peaks, while the Americans and Canadians were for the most part as fresh as paint, we did not do badly in Washington.

The chef d'équipe later stated that only O'Malley, Harvester and Carnaval of the British team started in the puissance because he did not want to jump the others 'in such a punishing event so early on in the tour'. I see things differently. My two were the only true puissance horses in the team. The others might make 6 feet 6 inches with a scramble but that was their lot whereas mine will jump that height with ease every time I take them to it. To a horse who can get height, a puissance competition is no more punishing than any straightforward one. Here at Washington both O'Malley and Harvester reached the third jump-off with Shapiro's Jacks or Better and Kathy's Aberali. The wall was raised to 6 feet 8 inches, which is low by normal standards but in fact was the equivalent of a greater height because it was very light-topped and would not stand even a flick. Jacks or Better refused before clearing it at the second attempt and Aberali hit it; so when my pair hopped over I recorded my first win in North America.

In the President's Trophy, the main contest of the show, only Night Spree and Vibart were clear first time, Night Spree eventually running out the winner with a second clear round. Harvester took off too far away from a wide parallel in the first round and, flattening out over the top, rolled a pole off. Still, third place was sufficient to clinch for him the titles of Grand Champion Jumper and International Champion Jumper as leading horse of the show. I got the sash as top international rider and the team totalled three wins, as against two each by the United States and Canada.

At the end of the Washington show, the British team made their various ways to New York, Irene and I flying there with Neil Shapiro in his private plane. Our base in New York was the vast, 3400-bed Americana Hotel, which was quite close to Madison Square Garden, home of the National Show for forty-one years. Coming from peace-loving England it was hard to realize that it was dangerous to make the short walk from the Garden to the hotel alone. A friend of mine had just set off to do that very thing when a squad car pulled up and gave him a stern warning not to go near the inside of the pavement. To do so, it seems, is to invite an attack. It is all car travel in New York, and I could see why.

The schedule at New York and, later, at Toronto, was an improvement on Washington, with national and international classes on the same night. The well-dressed crowd, among whom evening dress seemed to be the rule rather than the exception, had plenty to enjoy during each session.

The Americans started hot favourites for the Nations Cup. With a team made up of Night Spree (Neil Shapiro), a very, very good mare of true Olympic class, Untouchable (Kathy Kusner), who was right back to form after being off for a long time, Salem (Carol Hofmann) and Snowbound (Bill Steinkraus), they would have taken some beating had our horses been at their best and that we ran them to a jump-off was mainly due to the small course, over which there were clear rounds galore. In the unusual situation of a Nations Cup jump-off against the clock, the Americans made sure of victory after Salem went clear and Untouchable scored just four again.

One day of New York remained, containing the main contest of the show, the Grand Prix. Stage-planning had made this the last event to be held in this Madison Square Garden and there was a full house to cheer the anticipated American triumph. O'Malley had not been going well enough to have any real chance as things were so I stripped him of martingales for the first time in his jumping life, hoping that this would act as a form of shock treatment and make him pull out a bit extra. Arthur McCashin made a fair job of the course, especially as his scope was limited by not being able to use any bush filling because of fire restrictions, but still thirteen of the seventeen starters went clear first time – all six British horses, three Canadians and four Americans.

At one stage in the timed jump-off Canada were in first, second, and third places through Jimmy Elder's Pieces of Eight, Canadian Club and Big Dee, before Kathy, the last American to go, scorched round on Untouchable to go into the lead with a clear in 37.5 seconds. Stroller, Firecrest, Carnaval and Vibart each made one mistake and then Franco, who had been going better for Caroline Bradley than at any time in his career, jumped a first-rate round one second faster than Untouchable. Then it was O'Malley's turn to jump the last round of all in the huge stadium. We got on the right side for time by cutting inside a fence to reach the second obstacle, turned pretty sharp to the wall and after clearing the double I managed a quick glance at the clock, which was bang in line with me at that point. It told me we were okay, but I did not ease up and O'Malley pressed on to get a winning margin of 1.5 seconds. I suppose it was a case of 'the impossible' so dear to some writers.

The performance helped me to win the award for the leading foreign rider, Billy Steinkraus earning the most important one of leading international rider. His Bold

Minstrel had not touched a fence throughout the show. The team award went to the eight-horse American outfit.

After two days we journeyed up to Toronto for the Canadian Royal Winter Fair held on a massive site and with all the stabling, cattle sheds, schooling areas and the main arenas under one roof. I got round most of the show and enjoyed it immensely, especially sections like those for tropical fish and foreign birds, which are not to be found at the normal British county show.

Things were not promising for us as far as the jumping went because by the time we reached Toronto the horses had really gone off and to make matters worse all bar Firecrest and Franco developed some kind of kidney trouble which caused them to seize up in their backs.

I left Harvester out of the puissance at Toronto and relied on O'Malley to show his home crowd that he was still a good horse. It was exactly six years since he had won the individual championship at the Winter Fair. After the shock treatment at New York, I put a long running martingale on him which had no effect so long as he didn't turn his head, and he showed me in the first round that this was to be one of his better days. Up went the fences and again he was comfortably clear, along with four others, Ted on Carnaval, Kathy on Aberali, Crystine Jones on Trick Track, and Jim Day on Canadian Club. Carnaval and Aberali fell out at 6 feet 9 inches and after a successful go at 7 feet Trick Track was withdrawn, leaving O'Malley and Canadian Club to fight it out over a big parallel and the wall at 7 feet 3 inches. Canadian Club went first, popped over the parallel but stopped at the wall. He went over all right at the second attempt to beat the existing Canadian record, leaving me with a clear to win. From the word go O'Malley went like a winner and he gave the wall inches to spare.

The crowd liked it as first-rate entertainment, but once again voices were raised against the puissance and Colonel Llewellyn set down in print his strongly felt objections to 'fierce competition among a lot of horses limited to one big, heavy wall'. Later Colonel Sir Mike Ansell instigated a change in the conditions for the puissance class in Britain, making it less of a one-fence competition, but I was happy enough with the earlier arrangements.

For a start, we have to remember that show-jumping now depends on its ability to attract spectators and give good entertainment, and the puissance nearly always was good entertainment. Secondly, horses who can jump height do not take an undue amount out of themselves; and, thirdly, the wall is a much safer proposition than poles, sloping or otherwise. With a wall, horses meeting it wrongly, or those incapable of taking the height, either stop or have the odd brick out. I have seen very few cases where a horse has been really hurt tackling a wall. Not so with sloping poles. They need to be packed with filling to cut out the daylight and even then when a horse jumps into the middle of that kind of fence he often hurts himself badly.

In addition to the nobbling problem, the years 1966 and 1967 brought special attention to cruelty in show-jumping and, in particular, alleged blistering of the cannon bones and fetlocks of horses so that they were doubly likely not to hit a fence. An article in a leading national newspaper, claiming that this blistering was going on, prompted a whole series of allegations about the sport which are forever being repeated. It was said that 'rapping' (banned by the BSJA) was fairly common, that sometimes horses were badly beaten as a punishment for making jumping mistakes, that electric spurs were used to cause shocks and, again, punish mistakes, that horses were ridden round practice courses the wrong way so that if they hit a pole it would not fall out of its cup but would hurt the horses more than ever. And so on.

The BSJA took heed of the 'blistering' reports and, ever anxious to let the world see that they were keen disciplinarians, announced before Wembley 1966 that selected horses wearing bandages would be subject to a veterinary spot test after each competition during the six-day show. A statement by the director of the show, Colonel Ansell, said that he and his committee were confident that suggestions that a mild turpentine blister 'is a well-known means of teaching horses not to hit fences' were ill-founded and the checks were being made to provide evidence that their confidence was not misplaced.

The motive behind the spot checks cannot be criticized but if they really wanted to prove their point they should have kept quiet and so retained the element of surprise. Only a lunatic would have tried the dodge knowing a test was likely, and yet the BSJA got their man – or so they thought. The spot check was made on a horse on the Wednesday night: the bandages were unwrapped and the BSJA vet sent the cotton wool inside the bandages, and the bandages themselves, away for laboratory tests. The horse was immediately suspended from further jumping at the show and the threat of punishment then hung over the owner, there to stay until results of the tests came through the following week.

The owner protested that the liquid on the cotton wool had been a proprietary leg wash. After a competition the previous night he had applied the wash in the usual way to take any inflammation out of his horse's legs and on that fateful Wednesday he had examined them and then replaced the cotton wool inside the jumping bandage. 'My horse's legs,' he told the BSJA, 'are in perfectly good shape.'

Sensibly he took matters into his own hands and called in an independent veterinary surgeon for his opinion. He gave the horse a clean bill of health and the BSJA took no further action. I am not criticizing the BSJA for wanting to make sure that their sport is clean, but they have a remarkable capacity for doing the wrong thing at the wrong time.

That was not by any means the end of the 'turpentine' story. It will keep cropping up, I'm sure, and so I will explain a bit more about it. Those who started the allegations, and the BSJA, referred to a turpentine 'blister' – a blister caused by the application of the liquid inside bandages. But what it causes is a skin irritation, not a blister in the true sense of the word; its effect is similar to that of itching powder on human beings. It does, though, make the horse's skin tender and if he hits a pole in that condition he certainly knows he has hit one.

Every horse is different in physical qualities as well as character and the idea that all horses could have turpentine applied to their legs shows a total lack of understanding about them. If, for instance, Sea Hawk had been 'turped' I would not have been able to get him anywhere near a fence – his skin was already more tender than that of a horse done with turpentine. And the idea that 'turping' was common was wrong. I have seen it done only a few times and then by people who were trying to get quick results.

Any sport has its black sheep. In show-jumping these are among the up-and-coming brigade, who have heard the fantastic tales of how so-and-so got to the top and decide to try methods out for themselves; they do not occur among the leading riders. It is possible to see Saturday-afternooners punishing their horses for a bad round, perhaps making them go time and again over a fence, because they have not the common sense to realize this is going to ruin the horse, not improve him. And some do go in for 'poling' – hitting a horse on the legs with an ordinary jumping pole as they take a fence. This really does knock a horse's end in.

'Rapping', of which 'poling' is a form, has a long history and in show-jumping dates back to the old days when fences were really light and had a half-inch lath on top. If a horse hit a lath he could have it down and not realize it. The riders then decided they had to make sure that their horses jumped six inches higher than seemed necessary, and it was in those old days that 'rapping' and 'turping' flourished. Some riders took to breeding hedgehogs for their skins, which they used to nail round a pole. Just as children very soon realize that it is best not to pick up a hedgehog they see in the street or the garden, so horses very soon decide to give extra height to a fence covered with hedgehog skins. And when they find their legs being rapped with these sharp skins they try to give every fence extra clearance.

Even more painful 'rapping' instruments have been used.

Iron bars used to be common and the occasional stupid man used a pole with nails stuck in it. One brilliant present-day rider used regularly to school with a piece of tight wire above a pole. If a horse catches this it has a burning effect on the horse's shins. This method could have disastrous results if applied by the inexperienced.

The one country where 'rapping' is carried on openly and without any sense of guilt is the United States where they still stage 'rub' classes – classes in which horses touching a fence are penalized. The scene in the collecting ring before these national classes has to be seen to be believed. Even the top riders indulge in the tapping, back and front, of horses with a light cane. In the right hands there is nothing cruel in this and competitors are faced with the problem of keeping their horses extra sharp.

In Great Britain, apart from the BSJA's outlawing of 'rapping', there simply is no point in doing it. The courses are now so big and so wide that if a horse tries to give a fence six inches to spare he cannot get away with it. If a horse has gone sloppy on you and started to change his legs it is far better, to my mind, to put up a pole and say to him: 'Please yourself. If you hit it you will know about it: if you clear it you are all right.' For hitting a pole causes quite enough pain to a horse without adding extra discomfort.

What all those people who employ doubtful or cruel methods as a means of short-cutting their way up forget is that if you start ill-treating a horse he is not going to do his best for you. And at any level of show-jumping it is vital that horse and rider have each other's respect.

In all the fuss about jumping malpractices the one aspect that is neglected is bitting and it is in their mouths that show-jumpers suffer most of all. I have seen horses coming out of the ring with blood in their mouths as the result of bad hands, bad riding and curb bits. A curb gives a three to one pull on the mouth, and if a rider chops with his hands considerable force comes into it. A horse's mouth is extremely sensitive and this kind of treatment does cause bad pain. Stewards at shows should take action and tell guilty riders to cut it out.

But, for all the things that do go on which should not, I think the BSJA was foolish in the way it tackled the problem. There is too much money tied up in the good-class jumpers for any rider to start ill-treating them. So it is not at shows like the Horse of the Year that the extra vigilance, spot checks and the like, should come into play. It is at the small events populated by Saturday-afternooners. With very few exceptions the leading British riders set a good example of how to train and ride show-jumpers.

10. Mexico-bound

1968, the year of the Mexico Olympics, proved once again that planning for the big event is not the strong point of the BSJA. After the Tokyo shambles, there was much talk of a scheme that would produce the best possible horses and riders for Mexico, all at the top of their form.

The idea was that a short-list of candidates for the Olympics would be drawn up at the beginning of the season and that they should all compete against one another at certain national and international shows throughout the season. What they failed to take into account was that to jump at the first major event, Rome, each horse would have to be brought up in March. As the Olympics took place in September, it meant that the British team horses would have to be at the top of their form for eight months – far too long for most horses.

I remember arguing at the time that the way to produce a strong Olympic team was for the BSJA to trust their own judgement and pick four horses by 1 January of Olympic year. Then the horses need not be brought up until June, having got the best of the spring grass, when they could be taken on to compete at the Royal International and Dublin. After a concentrated period of work of about a month, the horses could then be eased off and kept semi-fit until they reappeared at one or two shows to sharpen up just before the big event.

The answer I got from one of the leading authorities in the Association when I warned them about the dangers of repeating the mistakes of Tokyo was predictable. 'Don't dig up the past.' I was told. The events of that year proved that British show-jumping had yet to learn from its mistakes.

But the season wasn't all bad news. Early in the year, Anneli Drummond-Hay and I travelled out to Berlin for the Berlin indoor show, which was and is the most competitive indoor show in Germany, closely followed by Dortmund, Frankfurt and Hanover. I had decided to take with me a brilliant, headstrong horse I had recently taken on at the request of his owner, Cecil Attwood. The idea was that I would take him around a few shows to see how we got on as he was a strong type and had proved a difficult ride until then. His name was Madison Time and he was to have a brilliant but tragically short career with me.

Madison Time went well at Berlin and, after a short spell at home I took him with O'Malley to s'Hertongenbosch, Frankfurt and Dortmund. O'Malley was trying to win the puissance at Dortmund for the third year in succession and I sensed relief all round among the other competitors when he went out at 6 feet 6 inches. What they didn't know was that I had another horse up my sleeve and in a close battle he was the only one left in the competition having cleared the wall at 7 feet 2 inches.

I was selected for the British team to go on to the Rome international show during the first week in May and decided to take Madison Time with Marney Peak who was a useful horse against the clock. The Gran Premio di Roma was the first major test for the Olympics, the course being built on the same lines, and it was this event that really put Madison Time into the reckoning for the Olympic team. The big course caused him no problems and eventually he scored a total of twelve faults for the two rounds to share fourth place with Stroller. All in all it was a good show for both of us: he helped the British team to second place in the Nations Cup and came equal second in the puissance while I ended up the leading rider of the show.

Madison Time was turning out to be a big horse with huge potential and I would have liked him to have had time to develop. But time and events were against us. At the beginning of the season I had assumed that Harvester would be my horse for Mexico and I had started him late in the season. He was not going well at Liverpool and again felt 'footy' at the outdoor Wembley show in the summer. As he was sometimes sore on his splints, I decided to send him back to Bert Cleminson to have them looked at. I never rode him again. Bert decided to hand him over to his son Ben and after that this horse who at his peak was one of the best in the world won very little.

Of my other horses I had ruled out Mattie Brown as an Olympic horse. Although he was going well he had a little too much respect for his fences to take on a big Olympic course. Madison Time was different, a real man's horse and so, despite his inexperience, I decided that he was my horse for Mexico.

The so-called short-list consisted of David Broome, Peter Robeson, Alison Dawes, Andrew Fielder, Althea Roger-Smith, Marion Coakes and myself and the selectors eventually chose David and Mister Softee, Marion with Stroller, Alison and The Maverick and myself with O'Malley and Madison Time to go to Mexico.

The short-term preparations for the Olympics were fortunately better planned than the selection procedure. As the Games would be held at 7000 feet above sea level the entire British equestrian team arrived in Mexico some time before the Olympics to allow us to acclimatize. The problems of exerting oneself at such a high altitude soon became apparent. I used to go for a run before breakfast and found that after a short sprint I would be fine for twenty seconds but would then find it almost impossible to breathe. As for the horses, a special feed was prepared for them and all the water they drank was purified.

The acclimatization period was a long one, but the British party worked well together. The team manager was Lieutenant-Colonel Harry Llewellyn and he and the team all got on well. Morale was already high when, shortly before our turn came, we heard that the British three-day event team had won the gold medal.

The individual Grand Prix took place on Wednesday, 23 October, and for the first time a new type of competition was used to decide the medals. Three competitors from each of the fourteen nations taking part would jump the first round over a course similar in type and size to a Nations Cup course. Then the leading horses would jump off over a shortened course which included jumps which would not have been out of place in a puissance event. The most daunting of these were a wall of 5 feet 11 inches and a diabolical parallel bars, 5 feet 7 inches high with a spread of more than 7 feet.

As we were drawn to go in last, I was forty-second to go into the ring. By the time my turn came round, there had been only two clears – Stroller and Bill Steinkraus on Snowbound. Madison Time had a couple down and went through to the jump-off over the big course. Stroller found the big parallel too big for him in the second round and had that and one other fence down. This kept him in the lead until Snowbound came in again. Steinkraus's horse put in an extraordinary performance as he was later found to be too lame even to be present at the prize-giving. Apart from faulting at the parallel bars he went clear to win the gold with a two-round total of four faults.

Madison Time came in with a chance of getting the bronze medal. I doubted whether he would clear the tricky parallel but, if this was the only fence he had down, he must be a contender for third place. In fact, he did have it down and also put a brick out of the wall which put paid to our chances of a medal. He finished seventh in the end and, remembering that until January that year he had won no competition of any significance, I was very satisfied with his performance.

David jumped-off for the bronze and after a brilliant round clinched it. The British had finished with second, third and seventh places and looked strong favourites for the Nations Cup – particularly as the American team had lost one of their best horses in Snowbound.

The course for the team event was a killer. It was not

the size of the fences – they were in fact smaller than for the individual event, but its length which seemed sure to find out a lot of horses at this altitude. To make things worse, the judges had imposed an impossible time limit so that, to avoid time faults, horses had to jump faster than their normal jumping speed.

Stroller was the first to go for Britain and, although he had one stop and time faults, his twenty-one and three-quarter faults kept us in the competition. After Madison Time had got round with eighteen and a quarter faults and Softee, one of the few horses to jump within the time limit, had collected eight, we were in the lead at the end of the first round. Canada was just behind us, France was third and Germany fourth.

As Marion went in for her second round, we all knew that, if Stroller was anywhere near his best, we were home. David and I had finished warming our horses up and were among the 100 000 crowd watching Stroller's fateful round. As soon as he had jumped the first fence, both of us sensed that something was wrong. The pony was jumping with none of his usual fluency. Sensing disaster, I quickly moved down to the edge of the ringside just in time to see them stop in the middle of the big treble. He refused a second time and this time Marion was unseated. When she got on again she headed for the exit until a few choice words from me sent her back for a third attempt. She cleared and finished the course, a brave performance but one which did us no good as she was eliminated for exceeding the time limit. The Canadians went on to win the gold medal.

Despite the disappointing end to the Games, Mexico had been a worthwhile experience for me. Apart from giving Irene and myself a good break from home, it had confirmed my opinion that in Madison Time I had a very good horse indeed.

By the next spring he was going even better. He picked up the Grand Prix at Hanover, the first major show of the 1969 season, won prizes at Dortmund and then came home to Hickstead where he jumped three clear rounds to win the Grand Prix, ending up the leading horse of the show. Madison Time had arrived.

A few weeks later I rode him at the Royal Windsor – his last show, as it turned out. After jumping a clear in the Supreme Championship he collapsed on the way out and was found to have died immediately. Apparently he had broken a blood-vessel during the round and had suffered an internal haemorrhage.

He was a great loss to me. He was not the easiest of horses to ride but, on his day, he had more ability than any other horse I've ridden. To lose him just as he was approaching his prime was a shattering blow.

Of my other horses, O'Malley continued to win his share of prizes. I had taken him on the American and Canadian circuits after Mexico and in New York he cleared 7 feet to win the puissance at the American National Horse Show. In the spring show at Dortmund, he once again showed what a good horse he was over big jumps when he won the puissance there. But, honest and hard as he was, O'Malley was finding the major events hard to win and from 1969 I used him more as a stop-gap than as one of my lead horses.

He did have one taste of glory, though. At Wembley in 1970, after Willie Halliday had begun to ride him for me, he was involved in a great two-horse battle for the Norwich Union puissance. His opponent was myself on Mattie Brown. When the wall reached 6 feet 6 inches, Mattie Brown cleared it and also the big spread that remained to be jumped. O'Malley got the wall but had the spread down to finish second.

Apart from that event, O'Malley had had a moderate season and when I was asked to let a girl called Pat Kaye have him for a year I readily agreed. He was placed with Pat in one or two classes before dying, like Madison Time, of a broken blood-vessel, when jumping a practice jump at home.

11. Getting my personality over

The men's world show-jumping championships held at La Baule in 1970 once again raised serious questions about the selection procedure adopted by the BSJA for big international events. First, as George Hobbs, David Broome and myself were all chosen for the two-man team, if George had not had the bad luck to break his wrist two days before the show at La Baule started, none of us would have known which of us was to be selected until just before the competition.

In addition, Beethoven, whom David had elected to ride rather than Top of the Morning, was an erratic performer who could beat the best horses in the world one day and fail to finish the course the next. A further complication was that he belonged to our chef d'équipe, Duggie Bunn – not the best arrangement to ensure that all horses in the team were treated equally.

I had my own problems. Two weeks before the championship Mattie Brown, whom I was to ride, started going lame from an old splint that had been troubling for a year or so. When we arrived at La Baule, I took him paddling in the sea and repeating this most days kept him sound for the show.

Of the twenty-seven starters for the three qualifying competitions, Alwin Schockemohle's great horse was firm favourite among the experts. The first event, a speed competition, was over a big course but this did not worry Mattie Brown. Despite putting a foot in the water, an error I have later found that horses often make after paddling in the sea, he did have the fastest round to lead the field by half a second from Donald Rex with David on Beethoven two seconds behind in third place.

The second qualifying event was a puissance in which ten horses, not including Beethoven who had one fence down, went through to the jump-off. Our main rival, Donald Rex, hit the parallel in the second round so that when Mattie Brown went clear again to share first place with Graziano Mancinelli's Fidux and Hugo Arrambide's Adagio he remained the leading qualifier.

A two-round competition over a Nations Cup type course was the final qualifying event, and it was here that Beethoven came through with the only double clear to win the competition and gain a place in the four-horse final. Mattie Brown had a fence down in both rounds but still ended the leader of those qualifying, followed by Mancinelli with Fidux, David with Beethoven and Alwin with Donald Rex.

The championship competition to be decided between the four of us was an unusual one. We were all to jump both our own horses and the other three competitors' horses. The winner is decided after four rounds. I have always thought that this type of competition was too gimmicky to be taken seriously – certainly it is a strange way to decide a world championship. First, it is open to all kinds of abuse and gamesmanship. For example, a rider on his own horse can stir him up a bit towards the end of his round so that he is unsettled and a handful for the other riders. Or it is easy to adjust the bridle in some way before the next competitor takes on your horse. Surely the best way to arrange a championship is a straight competition to decide the best horse-and-rider combination in the world.

The system at La Baule was to add a penalty of 25 per cent for faults incurred on your own horse, and this was to prove my undoing. Mattie Brown rolled one off in the first round and, as all the others had clears, I was soon five faults down.

The second horse I rode was Fidux. Mancinelli had made my job no easier by winding him up a bit towards the end of his round. As he was a big, strong horse, there was little more that I could do but steer, kick, check and hope and, after a particularly unsmooth round, we had four faults.

Beethoven I found a much easier ride but it was my final round on Donald Rex that gave me my most memorable moment of the show. As soon as I mounted, I knew I would have no problems with him and, once we started jumping, I realized why he had the reputation of being one of the best horses in the world. Everything he did was sheer poetry: when I checked him, he came back to me; when I asked him to shorten his stride, he shortened effortlessly. He was a tribute to Alwin's skill and training.

Unfortunately, by the time I rode Donald Rex, my chance of winning the championship had gone. Of the other three, David was the best rider on Mattie Brown, getting a clear round, while Mancinelli, who chopped at him all the way, collected four faults, and Alwin eight.

It was David's round on Donald Rex that clinched the championship. He had one fence down and this was good enough to win him the title from Graziano Mancinelli. I took third place and Alwin was fourth.

The following season, 1971, was an eventful one. Not only was there the famous episode at Hickstead (which I shall discuss later) which is still remembered in and out of show-jumping circles but I was also at the centre of considerable controversy on two other occasions, at Aachen and at Wembley's Horse of the Year Show.

Aachen took place in appalling conditions. Torrential rain had made the ground so heavy that, on some occasions, horses finished the course in a state of total exhaustion. I was riding Evan Jones at the show and, as he was only five at the time and had competed in the three-part European Championship only two days previously, he was getting a bit tired by the time I was asked to take him into the Nations Cup. In the circumstances, he did well enough with a first round of twelve faults. On our way out of the arena, I stopped him and reined him back. As he backed, his back feet stuck in the mud and he 'sat down' on his haunches. This unbalanced him and, panicking a bit, he threw himself over to one side unseating me in the process but not himself falling over. I got up and led him off. End of a trivial incident.

That was until I saw the following Sunday's *Sunday Times*. Under an article headed 'Show-jumping must come clean about this' were a series of photographs showing Evan Jones down on his hocks, then twisting sideways and finally me falling off. The caption, entitled 'Smith getting his personality over', described how I had pulled the horse over and then quoted Major Paul Weier, captain of the Swiss team at Aachen, as saying that after the incident I had remounted Evan Jones and 'hit him many times about the head. Afterwards, he took the horse into the practice field and jumped him backwards and forwards over the practice fence, maybe forty times. It was not gentlemanly.' The article ended with the question, 'Where should the line be drawn?'

The facts, it later turned out, were these: I never carried a stick when riding Evan Jones (as is proved by the photograph); I have always believed that 'the line should be drawn' before a rider hits his horse over the head once, let alone forty times; Paul Weier later denied ever having made the statement; the photographer had taken an amusing but totally insignificant series of pictures; and the reporter had acted on totally misleading information.

The inevitable BSJA enquiry followed and all these facts were established. Patrick Connolly-Carew, the Irish chef d'équipe, who had seen the incident, and the Aachen authorities testified that no cruelty was involved and I was completely cleared. The *Sunday Times* failed to report the result of the enquiry, prompting me to turn their own question on them: where *should* the line be drawn?

Apart from the incident, the Aachen European Championship went reasonably well for me. The two British representatives were Michael Saywell, with Hideaway and The Lodger, and myself, with Mattie Brown and the inexperienced Evan Jones. After the first two competitions of the three to decide the championship, I shared the lead with

Hartwig Steenken and two Swiss riders, Max Hauri and Paul Weier, were in third and fourth places.

We had to choose one horse each for the final, deciding event, and, bearing in mind the plough-like conditions of the course, I opted for the youth and strength of Evan Jones rather than the experience of Mattie Brown.

It was a two-round contest and there was only one clear in the first round by a Hungarian rider, Ajtonyl on Ozike. In the second round, my main rival, Steenken on Simona, went clear except for a refusal at the wall which meant that Evan Jones had to go clear to win the championship for me. He jumped brilliantly but his lack of experience found him out at the combination where he had one fence down.

I finished second in the championship to Hartwig Steenken with Paul Weier in third place and, in spite of my disappointment at not being European champion, I was delighted by Evan Jones's performance.

Back in England, I found myself once again providing work for the scribblers and the cartoonists. This time, it all happened at the British Jumping Derby meeting at Hickstead and the event which caused the controversy was a certain sign that I made at the end of the big event.

Mattie Brown was defending the title that he had won in 1970 and, although he had been troubled with a splint earlier in the 1971 season and had not yet quite found his form, I was confident that we would be keeping the Derby trophy.

It was not through confidence that I didn't bring the trophy with me but through sheer forgetfulness. When he found out that I had left the trophy at home, Duggie Bunn, the owner and manager of Hickstead, was furious. On the Friday before the Derby, which was on the Sunday, he came up to me and said, 'You will get that trophy back.' Now anyone who knows me will testify that the sure way not to get something done is to order me. It's not so much that I'm against authority as that I have never been able to stand people riding me. This dates back to my schooldays when I was often kept in after the final bell and always on the following morning was that much later to school.

A reporter who overheard my conversation with Bunn asked me if I thought I would be taking the trophy back with me. Before I could answer, Bunn said 'No chance', and walked off. Later I saw the sponsors of the Jumping Derby and the problem of the trophy was sorted out in no time.

As was usual with the Derby, the fences were rather bigger than in the previous year's event. I am not keen on Hickstead, as the course tends to confuse some horses. This is particularly true of the famous Hickstead bank which I have never liked, even when the slope was made less steep after Ann Backhouse's Chamusca Lad had broken a leg there.

The bank held no terrors for Mattie Brown, who was handier and more surefooted than many bigger horses, but it was the Devil's Dyke, a combination fence with the second part up a slope, which I thought could cause us problems. It was this fence that led to the V-sign incident.

I was a bit worried that Mattie Brown hadn't the stride to get out of the other side of the combination and, taking him into it too steadily, I allowed him to have the first part down. As the pole fell, I remember hearing a cheer going up from the stand by the getting which not only surprised me as I continued but also made me determined more than ever to win the Derby.

The cheer, as it turned out, had been a bit premature. Mattie Brown was the only horse among the twenty-seven starters to have only one fence down. Stephen Hadley on Prospero had a refusal and one time fault to give him four faults as well so that we had to jump-off.

Prospero had to jump-off first over a shortened course which did not include the bank and he had three fences down. But the competition was far from over. Mattie Brown had very little time to recover from his first round and was still blowing hard when we entered the ring after Prospero. Early on in the round he rolled a pole off and, when he followed this by having the gate down, I found I

only had one fence in hand. He jumped the rest of the course
clear.

As I circled him after finishing the course, I felt an enormous sense of relief and triumph and, on the spur of the
moment, raised two fingers – a V for victory – in the direction of the balcony. It was meant as a gesture of triumph
but if those spectators on the balcony who wanted me to
lose interpreted it differently, that was up to them. The
important thing for me was that Mattie Brown had become
the first horse to win the British Jumping Derby in successive
years.

After receiving the laurel wreath, I took Mattie Brown
back to his box and had a vet look at his splint. I left Hickstead in the horse box at eight in the evening unaware that
the press had already been fed the biggest sports story for
some time.

Driving home in the horse box, we got a double puncture
and had to send for a mechanic from a local garage. Hearing where we were coming from, the young man said, 'Oh
yes, where that horse was disqualified.' At the time, I
assumed that he was talking about another horse but, driving
into the yard early next morning, I soon heard the news.
I had been disqualified by the Hickstead stewards from
winning the Derby with its world-record prize of £2000 for
what they called 'disgusting behaviour'.

The telegram from Duggie Bunn on behalf of the show's
directors arrived at lunchtime and by then the press were
in full cry. During the morning there was a full-scale in-
vasion. I was not at my most diplomatic. The only way that
Bunn could make his accusation stick was by proving that
the gesture was a serious insult to the judges, and the
reaction of the crowd who cheered me out of the ring
showed that it had been a jokey, light-hearted incident.

The BSJA quickly ordered an enquiry to consider the
Hickstead's stewards' claim that I had acted in contraven-
tion of one of the show's rules which prohibits 'acts of dis-
courtesy and disobedience'. Facing not only disqualification
but also a year's suspension from the Association, I went

to the enquiry at Stoneleigh. The first hearing was adjourned
since the crucial BBC film of the event had been delayed in
the post and this caused me some relief. I found that the
Hickstead stewards were to be legally represented and
decided that for the second hearing I should also have a legal
adviser.

My choice was Ron Rumsey, who understood show-
jumping and knew the law. At the hearing the committee
of enquiry eventually dismissed the case and recommended
that I should receive the £2000 prize. After the enquiry Ron
Rumsey and myself stayed behind to talk with Bunn about
the money and we agreed that a proportion of the prize
should be given to the Riding for the Disabled Fund.

The incident has done me more good than harm. At
Wembley, when winning the Foxhunter Championship, I
gave the V-sign as I left the ring. The crowd gave me one
of the best receptions I have ever had.

12. Destination Munich

My young horse Evan Jones went on improving through 1971 despite his gruelling ordeal in the mud at Aachen. A measure of his improvement was his increase in winnings. When I bought him as a four-year-old in 1970 he had won a total of £234, the biggest prize of which was £35 won at the North Wales Show. By the end of 1971, his winnings stood at £1650, an extraordinary achievement considering he had won hardly anything before June that year.

At the Horse of the Year Show he won the Cortina Crown and was also at the centre of the third controversy in which I was involved in 1971. It was after the Leading Show Jumper of the Year competition in which Mattie Brown had been fourth and Evan Jones sixth. As I rode into the ring for the presentation, a photographer asked me to jump a fence. Noticing that the op pole of the first part of the combination had been taken down, I popped Evan Jones over it as we left the ring.

Unwittingly I had caused another 'incident'. I was told by the ground jury that I had contravened an article in the FEI (Fédération Equestre Internationale) rule book forbidding competitors to jump obstacles in the ring except when competing. I came up in front of the jury and after the photographer concerned had backed up my story I was cleared.

But that was not the end of the affair. A group of people, represented by George Hobbs, chairman of the BSJA Rules Committee, lodged an objection to the jury's decision, claiming that they had been wrong to apply an international rule to a national competition. Not only should I be disqualified from the Leading Show Jumper of the Year competition, they said, but I should forfeit all the prize money I had won in the previous four days. Once again, the BSJA had to hold a hearing and, under the chairmanship of Duggie Bunn, the committee decided that the ground jury had been wrong to apply international rules and they were reprimanded. Incidentally, the FEI in Brussels finally decided that the BSJA had been wrong in this case and the reprimand had to be withdrawn.

Towards the end of 1971, the BSJA selectors were already considering candidates for the Munich Olympics the following year. Evan Jones was not being considered, partly because of his performance in the Nations Cup at Aachen and partly because he was not the selectors' idea of an Olympic horse. It was true that, to look at, he was just a little Welsh cob, but he had all the spring and ability of a thoroughbred and was careful with it.

The type of horse that makes a successful show-jumper has changed enormously over the years. When the fences were mostly upright, big, heavy cobs were right for the job, but today's courses, which demand horses that can jump a big spread, pick themselves up and take a stride and stretch again, would soon find them out.

Although Evan Jones was out, both Archie and Johnny Walker were on the first short-list and they were soon joined by Summertime who was also coming good during the 1971 season.

I had first noticed Summertime in 1965 when Sheila Barnes was riding him. Since then he had had a checkered jumping career but had won some good prizes with Ted Williams and later Mike Saywell, who rode him for Trevor Banks.

My first show with Summertime was in December 1970 at Zuidlaren in Holland, where he jumped well without winning any of the major competitions. The following spring I took him to Dortmund where the Aachen course-builder, Hans Brinckmann, put up a course for the championship of Dortmund designed to sort us all out.

Nine horses went clear, including two of the greatest horses in the world, Simona and Donald Rex, and Summertime. Simona did another clear in the fast time of 30.9 seconds, but Summertime surprised them all by clipping 1.3 seconds off that time, again going clear. Donald Rex failed to match our time but pushed Simona into third place.

As the season wore on, I had less trouble with Summertime's one trouble – a tricky mouth. I found that if I didn't touch his mouth he wouldn't throw his head in the air and unbalance himself. By the Easter meeting at Hickstead, we had more or less got over this problem and he had a great show, winning both the £1200 Wills Grand Prix from The Maverick and open points championship for the leading horse of the show.

He continued to improve and by the spring of 1972 I was convinced that, as long as I left his mouth alone, he could beat the best in the world. By now, I was riding him in an ordinary snaffle with a drop noseband and he went very well in this.

After putting in some good performances at the Continental spring shows, he came to Frankfurt to win the first four classes off the reel ending up the leading horse of the show.

The strategy for selecting the British team for Munich had been worked out by the selectors, headed by their chairman, Colonel Harry Llewellyn. There were to be two official trials, at the Bath and West Show and the Royal Highland, and the horses on the short-list were not to travel abroad too much in the first part of the season. Later it was decided that there should be other trials at the Great Yorkshire Show and Hickstead.

I missed the Bath and West, where the trial was won by Sweep from Pennwood Forge Mill, but went to the Royal Highland. The course might have been designed for Summertime as it included a tricky combination, which was his speciality, and he won the trial after being the only horse to jump two clear rounds. The selectors added him to the short-list.

In the third of the trials at Harrogate's Great Yorkshire Show I rode Summertime, Evan Jones, and Volvo, a young horse I had bought in 1971 who had all the makings of a top-class international show-jumper. This time it was Hideaway who showed us the way home after jumping the only clear round.

Summertime continued to jump brilliantly throughout the summer and I was greatly looking forward to the final Olympic trial at Hickstead. Evan Jones put himself out of the competition – and the reckoning for Munich – by making silly mistakes and having four fences down. Summertime put a foot in the water, a mistake for which I blamed myself as he was one of the best jumpers of water I have ever ridden. Eventually he came in fourth behind Hideaway, Manhattan and Psalm and in front of Pennwood Forge Mill, The Maverick and Sweep.

As soon as the event was over, the selectors got together to choose the team for Munich. I heard who was going to be in the team from Ann Moore's father, Norman. None of the selectors had bothered to tell me that they had picked Hideaway, The Maverick, Psalm and Manhattan.

As fate would have it, this was not the end of the story. Shortly after Wembley, Alison Dawes wrote to the selectors requesting that The Maverick be dropped from the team since a slight injury had held him up at a critical point in the run-up to Munich. The selectors hurriedly met again and this time voted by four votes to three in favour of Summertime.

But there were further obstacles on my road to Munich. At Hull Show I helped my two sons, Stephen and Robert, get ready for their competition and was putting up a fence for them when a pony came into the fence from the oposite direction. I didn't see it coming and was hit by the pole it knocked off. It didn't knock me down but made me feel pretty rough for a while. After riding Mattie Brown in another competition I felt even worse.

I went into a private nursing home and was later told that I had ruptured a kidney, which meant that I could not ride for another two months. I told the specialist who was dealing with me that I still planned to ride in the Olympics and, although he obviously thought me touched in the head, he did not stand in my way.

Six or seven days later, defying advice from the specialist, I decided that I ought to get out of bed and start moving. After a very shaky start, I began to get in an hour or so's exercise a day and after ten days in the nursing home was on my way home. I was back at Craiglands Farm on a Tuesday. On the Thursday I decided it was time to get back in the saddle and sat on Summertime for ten minutes. We had a jump or two on the Friday and on Saturday I took him to a show at Doncaster.

Although I felt far from right and apparently looked as white as a sheet, I soon 'clicked in' again, winning the Open on Summertime and taking third prize on Volvo.

After that I knew that I was going to be able to do myself, my horse and the team justice in the Olympics. I was back on the road to Munich.

13. Turning-point

The Olympic village at Munich was a complex of concrete buildings which housed the twelve thousand competitors from all over the world in comfortable, if not luxurious, conditions.

The male members of the show-jumping team – Peter Robeson, Mick Saywell, myself and Ronnie Massarella, the team manager – had a flat to themselves while Ann Moore stayed in a separate building with the women athletes. The morale among the team was as good as it was on my first trip abroad to Dublin and much of the credit for this must go to Ronnie Massarella.

The individual Grand Prix was to take place ten days after our arrival in Munich at the Riem Equestrian Centre. The seventeen nations competing were allowed to field teams of three and I was disappointed but not totally surprised to hear that I was to be left out of the British team. Once again, the selection was handled badly and the press heard the news some five hours before I was told.

The course for the individual event was built by Brinckmann and was the best and fairest that has been seen for many Olympics. Heroes of the day, as far as the British were concerned, were Ann Moore and Psalm who, after going clear in the first round, made a mistake at the big combination in the jump-off and finished with eight faults, the same as Graziano Mancinelli's Ambassador and Neil Shapiro on Sloopy. In the final round, Psalm remembered the bad mistake he had made earlier and lost his nerve at some big upright rails. That refusal cost Ann the gold as Ambassador went clear. Sloopy then came in and brought two fences down so Ann had won the silver medal – a great achievement for her first Olympics.

The team Grand Prix was on the last day of the Games and, as each team was to have four members, we were all taking part. For the first time the competition was to be based on the best three scores of each team for the two rounds.

My first round with Summertime showed that both of us were short of competition practice. He made one or two silly errors and so did I and we ended up with sixteen faults. Of the others, Manhattan was at his best and had only four faults, Hideaway had eight and Psalm had eleven so it was Summertime's score that was discounted. Our total was twenty-three faults and, after the first round, we were in equal third place with Spain after West Germany who led with sixteen and the United States with sixteen and a quarter.

Next time round, we fought back. Summertime did a brilliant round and had only one down. Hideaway was next in and came out with eight faults. If Manhattan and Psalm did good rounds, we had a fighting chance of getting the gold. Sadly, Psalm's nerve went and Manhattan also jumped badly so that we were out of the running for the main two places. Eventually the Germans squeezed home by a quarter of a fault from the Americans and we were pipped for third place by the Italians.

Looking back, I think Summertime did well in the 1972 Olympics but if he had put in what he was capable of putting in he would have done even better, and he had the ability to win the individual title. Unfortunately, as I knew at the time, he didn't really like the job and was resentful of having to work for a living. What I didn't know was that Munich 1972 would be my last opportunity to win an Olympic gold medal.

Not long after Munich, I became the first British rider to announce that I was going to become a professional. Other leading riders followed suit, some by choice, some because they were made to do so. Ted Edgar, David Broome, Paddy McMahon and Caroline Bradley are four of the top riders who were not given any choice by the BSJA, who had set up an executive committee to study professionalism in show-jumping.

Prince Philip, as president of the Fédération Equestre Internationale, stated at their meeting in December 1972 that unless show-jumping organizers controlled their amateurs and professionals there was a strong possibility that show-jumping would be turned out of the Olympic movement. Britain, he said should take the initiative and make so-called 'semi-amateurs' turn professional.

Colonel Harry Llewellyn followed by stating that his British Association was going to 'make it quite clear who is amateur and who is professional'. He added: 'We may be out on our own for a year but others will follow. It is imperative that all federations should take a firm stand. Now is the time, when no Olympic Games are imminent, to put our house in order.'

I thought at the time that Harry Llewellyn was right, and that after putting their own house in order the BSJA could go after the others, in particular Germany, where up to 70 per cent of their top riders were, in reality, professionals. Some of them had been paid by the state for years; others had fictitious jobs, as car-park attendants and so on.

That would have been all very well if things had gone according to plan and the other major show-jumping nations had followed the British example as they were supposed to. They didn't and, at the time of writing, still have not done so, making Britain the laughing-stock of the show-jumping world. While David, Paddy and myself will have to sit on the touchline at Montreal, the Germans and the rest will be fielding their strongest teams. Yet many of the competitors are just as professional as we are.

If we wanted to, we could take the lid off the pro-amateur situation and give evidence which would sink other nations, but I would prefer to open doors, not shut them. We should wait until all riders become, not amateurs and professionals, but simply show-jumpers. In my opinion

E

the sooner this happens the better, and the sooner that all athletes are able to compete in the Olympic Games, irrespective of any so-called professionalism, the better. The fact that a man is getting paid to run 100 metres cannot make him any faster than one who is not getting paid. As things are now, athletes the world over are getting paid in various ways and still are able to compete in the Olympics.

And where does this leave the British? What chance has a fellow got who is working all day and training at night, against the full-time athletes of the Iron Curtain countries or the athletes on scholarship courses at American universities? None, because he is creased before he goes out training.

The Olympic Games must be thrown open to everyone, with the only qualification the athletic ability of the candidate. Until that happens show-jumping should have a world championship and a European championship on alternate years and should forget about the Olympic Games.

As far as my own position was concerned, I could make a living without show-jumping, but I felt that as I had given so many years of my life to amateur show-jumping and because I could go no further in England where I was at the top of the tree, it was time that I capitalized on what I had achieved.

I went on the look-out for someone to manage my non-show-jumping affairs, for with an agent handling my affairs I could keep things rolling with fewer shows. Financially I should be a lot better off: as an amateur I could not endorse products and I could not sell horses on any scale. I found John Marshall, an agent connected with show business.

Our plan was that he should sign myself, Nelson Pessoa, Alwin Schockemohle and Captain Raimondo d'Inzeo as four members of a professional team. Unfortunately Raimondo decided to stay with the Carabinieri and Alwin, an industrialist and a wealthy man in his own right, was persuaded to keep himself available for the German Olympic team. As a result, our plans for the first international professional show-jumping team never got off the ground.

14. Enter Trevor Banks

At the time that I announced my decision to go professional there was plenty of publicity about the proposed team, and it was said by leading members of the press who were not in favour of the idea that I had 'not exactly shone' during the 1972 season.

In fact, although I had not had a horse to share the top spot with Summertime, I did have two horses in the BSJA Top Ten for international and national winnings. Summertime was runner-up to Pennwood Forge Mill, who was figuring in the list for the first time, and Evan Jones was tenth. Summertime's placing meant that I had been in the first five for five successive years and, overall, I was well ahead of anyone else in Britain.

I also had a horse coming up who I felt sure would soon break the big time. He was Salvador, a big Hanoverian. Paul Schockemohle, a younger brother of Alwin, had had him as a four-year-old and he showed a lot of promise. Paul did not join the German team until 1971 and, when he owned Salvador, he was doing more dealing than show-jumping. Alwin gave Paul £10 000 for Salvador, plus two other horses. Paul worked on the two bad ones, one of whom turned out to be Askan, which he sold for £56 000, and the other Amateur, who went on to win a lot of big puissance events. In other words, Alwin bought Salvador for around £70 000.

He let other riders have Salvador for a couple of years and he didn't win a thing. He was napping and wouldn't go, even for Alwin. I talked to Alwin at Rotterdam in 1972, when Salvador was a six-year-old, and he told me he was sick of the horse – so sick, in fact, that he gave half of the horse to me.

Salvador had a will of his own as all his riders had found out to their cost. I got him in September and did a little bit with him, taking him down to Burghley, and he started to get into the money, I had seen him jump in odd shows and knew that he was a funny-tempered horse with a real mean streak in him. But I got him thinking my way and the following January I started him in the Grades A and B event which was a supporting contest to the Martell International Grand Prix at the Harewood indoor arena in Essex. It came down to a six-horse jump-off against the clock and Salvador won easily from True Lass, ridden by Caroline Bradley. Ted Edgar was third on Everest Peak and David Broome was fourth on Sportsman, so the form was useful.

Not long after that I set off for Berlin with him and Summertime. I jumped Salvador in all the big classes and he started off well by having only one down in the first round of the Preis von Deutschland, a two-round affair. He went clear in the second round to take fourth place. Jean Michel Gaud and Tango, a horse who later did well at Wembley, had the only double clear to win.

The 1973 home season got off the mark with the Easter meeting at Hickstead, held in typical holiday weather with rain and bitterly cold winds. The ground was deep and treacherous by the Monday and I took it steady on Salvador in the six-horse jump-off for the Grand Prix. He went clear but collected a time fault. That was good enough for second place, the only one to better Salvador's total being Flipper with Hugo Simon.

During this Hickstead Trevor Banks and I announced that we were going into partnership. Trevor is a top-class dealer and it took the dealing side out of my hair, giving me more time to ride and school the horses. This is what I enjoy, as well as training and schooling riders; Trevor enjoys the dealing side so we thought it would work well.

For years and years before we joined forces Trevor was

just another one who couldn't stand being hammered. He had tried buying horses, he had tried buying jockeys, he had tried everything and still I was beating him. It really got at him so much that if I was doing a deal he would do his best to stop it going through. Eventually I started doing the same to him and our relationship deteriorated from one of mutual dislike to outright hatred.

The change began one day at the Royal Show. I was asleep in the wagon and Trevor came flying in and accused me of upsetting one of his deals. 'Yes,' I replied, 'that's right,' and another row was under way.

It seemed like stalemate until Trevor said that he would not upset any more of my deals. I agreed straight away not to upset any more of his and, slightly surprised by the turn of events, we shook hands on it. Off he went. About an hour later I was going into the ring to walk the course when I saw Trevor sitting out on his wagon ramp having a cup of tea.

'Seeing as you're my mate, you'd better have a cup of tea,' he said. Things built up from there until, after a fair amount of preliminary discussion, we made the partnership announcement at Hickstead.

Our first season together, 1973, was not a total success in or out of the ring, but it was not to be expected to be. Still Summertime was third in the BSJA Top Ten for national and international winnings and Salvador was only one place behind. Only Manhattan finished in front of Summertime in the international list.

Trevor's place is at Bishop Burton, not far from Beverley in the East Riding of Yorkshire. He has a set of horses there – around fifteen or so – and I have a set at my place, usually twenty-five or more. At the time that we started in partnership he had Hideaway, a top-class horse, and I took him over though he was never stabled with me. At his second show with me he won the Vauxhall Viva Stakes, incorporating the Area International Trial, at the Cheshire County. He was second to Beau Supreme in the AIT at the Three Counties Show and won the Crawford Scotch Whisky

Championship, from Trevarrion and Buttevant Boy, at the Royal Highland.

Another win followed at the Nottinghamshire Show Jumping Spectacular and then, at the Royal, he and Grebe were the only two to go clear over a big track for the Equizole Trophy. Grebe, going second in the jump-off, won with another clear to four faults, but it all added up to the biggest money-winning streak of Hideaway's life. And yet, because I was not able to spend enough time with him, he was not going as I would have liked.

There is no substitute for spending time with a horse, even if you are only leading him out on a halter: you are getting to know him. If you take him out for a bit of walking exercise, it is always a good idea to keep getting on him. The finest thing you can do with any horse is put him in a stable and then get him out again. Get him familiar with you, let him know that everything is okay. The trouble with Hideaway is that Trevor tends to treat him as a big baby and likes to wrap him up in cotton wool.

When I have spent some time with a horse and I collect him he must coil up like a spring and bounce on the spot. Hideaway didn't. He used to stick his nose out and put his back-end out the other way and get longer instead of getting more compressed with more power to get higher. It was like working a digger and pulling the wrong lever.

It wasn't long before we decided that it was better for Hideaway to have another jockey. Because Trevor had lost his stable jockey I let him have Paul Darragh, and he took over and did well. Trevor had started to interfere with my riding of Hideaway – 'Do it this way, do it that way' – which was something I had never had in my life. All I need when I am warming a horse up is for someone to tell me how he is jumping: is he tight in front? Is he dragging his hind legs? This niggling began to affect me and my riding. I was used to working out problems for myself and never welcomed other peoples' solutions. Trevor soon realized that I was better left alone on these occasions.

These were just the teething troubles of our partnership.

Things improved a lot after that first season and now we are, I think, one of the most powerful show-jumping outfits the world has seen.

Before I started with Hideaway, I went with the British team to Rome where we won the Nations Cup. Five of the nine countries represented had full teams at the show and there was a fair turnout for the Nations Cup. We led at the end of the first round. Summertime had one down, and so did Lionel Dunning on Arran Blaze, but April Love was clear with Ann Moore. April Love made a mess of it next time but Summertime went clear and so did Grebe. Arran Blaze had two down, to leave us clear of the Italians and the Dutch. A weakened German team was fourth.

Bandalero and Lights Out were winning with me at that time but when it came to the Men's European Show Jumping Championship at Hickstead in July it was with Salvador and Hideaway that I was chosen, along with Paddy McMahon, who had Pennwood Forge Mill and Pennwood Mill Bridge. Salvador had just begun his season. Hideaway was jumping good first rounds but, in my book, was not fit enough to get the second rounds. They have to be hard and fit in top competition and he was some way short of being right yet.

The first round was a speed test over a fairly big track. Hideaway would have been joint fourth if he hadn't had the first part of the treble down and so he dropped to eighth place behind Forge Mill. The second leg was a two-round competition, on Nations Cup lines. There was only one clear and that was by Hideaway in the first part. He was tired in the second and slipped from first to equal tenth having four fences down. Salvador had three down in all to share second place with Forge Mill and four others.

Hideaway had one of the two clears in the first part of the final competition and his time was so good in what was a speed test that he led at the halfway stage. He needed to keep his lead to bring me up to second place in the championship overall but had two down in the last part to drop me to sixteen and a half points, the same mark as Vittorio Orlandi of Italy, and Hugo Simon. Paddy was the clear winner, from Alwin Schockemohle. Third, a point and a half in front of me, was Hubert Parot, of France.

From Hickstead, we went straight on to the Royal International Horse Show – and to near disaster. During Salvador's round in the *Horse and Hound* Cup, we were approaching the fourth fence when I felt his hind legs give way beneath him and we crashed into the fence. What had happened was that the floorboards had given way as Salvador had taken off and his legs had slipped through. Neither of us suffered any damage and Colonel Sir Mike Ansell, the show director, offered a proportion of the prize money as compensation, which was very fair. Salvador later took the most valuable class – the £1200 John Player Trophy – by outpacing The Robber, ridden by Alwin Schockemohle, in the jump-off. It was the sixth time I had won the Royal International Grand Prix.

The Horse of the Year Show saw Summertime and Salvador well in the money but several of the biggest classes went abroad. Hugo Simon won the *Daily Telegraph* Cup on Flipper after Summertime had jumped one of his fastest clears and Flipper also took the Victor Ludorum. Hugo is not very big and is not the greatest stylist in the world but he has so much aggression and is so determined that he comes through a big winner. Against the clock, he is a formidable rival.

The Germans had a good team going well, as they usually have. They are clever tacticians, because they stick to the same horses and riders all the time. The German team is picked from between six and eight riders and they don't try to go on too broad a front. Thus they get better results. Any good horse which comes up in Germany finds its way to the team, whereas in England a good horse can be jumping for years and it may never get to the team.

Salvador and Lights Out went with me to the United States towards the end of October 1973 and both were winners in New York. Salvador won the Democrat Cup from Buttevant Boy, and Lights Out scored in a $1000 speed class in which Ballywillwill was second. Salvador also helped the team to win the Nations Cup in New York for the first time, having only one fence down in the two rounds. With Buttevant Boy, Beau Supreme and Sportsman all chipping in with clears, we had a fence to spare over the Germans and Americans. I ended up as leading foreign international rider and with the international individual championship.

The year 1974 began and ended well for me. Volvo won both the Grand Prix and the Victor Ludorum in Berlin in late January. Harvest Gold, who had been ridden by Willie Halliday at Wembley, rounded things off well at Amsterdam by winning a 'have-a-gamble' and the Grote Prijs van Nederland, which carried a Fiat 128 sports coupé as a prize as well as the money. Along with David Broome and Ted Edgar, I gave Hickstead a miss in the spring because it wasn't worthwhile financially to make the trip but I was there for the Derby meeting.

Salvador had not been going very well in the early part of the show. When a horse is going well you are apt to underwork him and to think that his job is finished once he has been in the ring. He is then getting only quarter of an hour to twenty minutes' work a day whereas he is used to having an hour and a half. Do that for a week and you suddenly find that your horse becomes a bundle of fire and is really on top of himself. Then you have to bring him back to earth and make sure that he gets out for an hour before a class, exercising and settling down.

Salvador was right again by Derby day and he went well through the first round to join Graham Fletcher's Buttevant Boy in the jump-off. Graham was drawn to go first on Buttevant Boy and had two down. I wasn't worried when Salvador hit the parallels because he hit them hard and if he ever hits a fence hard he never hits another for a while. I had Buttevant Boy on time, so I was home and dry for my third British Jumping Derby.

Winning the Jumping Derby means more to me than winning any other class simply because it carries more prize money than any other class in England. I'm jumping six and seven days a week and that bit of extra effort on Derby day just isn't noticed.

Behind the scenes at Hickstead, Duggie Bunn had unknowingly helped me to my third Derby. The saddle on which I usually rode Salvador was rubbing his back and causing him discomfort, so I borrowed one from Duggie's groom. It did the trick perfectly.

As Hickstead showed, Salvador was improving all the time. Such was his strength that he was jumping as easily at the end of the gruelling Derby course as he was at the beginning. Whereas Mattie Brown had to put everything in to jump this course, Salvador just took it in his stride.

Salvador's strength had been proved at the World Show Jumping Championship which had taken place earlier in the season at Hickstead. He had been eleventh in the thirteen-fence first round and reached the jump-off in the second leg, over a course of eight fences described as 'puissance type'. That moved me up to sixth place but twelve faults in the final section left me in seventh place, one behind Paddy McMahon and two behind David Broome, the other British riders. So the final stage was fought out by Hartwig Steenken, Eddie Macken, Frank Chapot and Hugo Simon.

Their horses, Simona, Pele, Main Spring and Lavendel, did nothing for the rest of the season. Neither did twenty-three of the other twenty-five horses, the exceptions being Salvador and Sportsman. They were the only two which this particular world championship did not knock out. Mrs Pamela Carruthers was presented with the Course Designer of the Year award for her world championship courses at a BSJA lunch at the back-end of the year yet, in my opinion, some of those fences she built at Hickstead were almost unjumpable.

Salvador managed to keep his form and at the Royal International was part of a British team which had a zero score in the Nations Cup. He also won the *Daily Mail* Cup – the Victor Ludorum – with nearly five seconds to spare over Philco, the best of David Broome's three horses in the jump-off.

Sportsman was in the Wembley team and, later, in the team at Dublin where we again beat the Germans and Americans. Salvador had a double clear and our score of three quarters of a time fault carried the day. Salvador continued to go well and a successful Horse of the Year Show helped to make sure that he ended the year as the biggest British money-winner. Jagermeister (formerly Manhattan) headed him in the international list but nothing was near him for national earnings. Despite having a long rest in the summer, Volvo was seventh for international winnings and tenth overall, so that once more I had two in the Top Ten.

There were other horses to be pleased about. Olympic Star, who won the Foxhunter Championship at Wembley – and landed me a bet of £300 to £30 – could be another Harvester; Speak-Easy was improving quickly and Askan, who joined Trevor and me in the summer, had promised not to stop any more.

There was and is plenty to look forward to.

15. A black eye from Jackie Pallo

I was entering my twentieth season in the top flight of show-jumping when I found that my enthusiasm for the sport was beginning to wear a bit thin. A lot of enjoyment seemed to have gone out of competing – I couldn't bear to talk horses at night and I even found my concentration was wandering in the ring. I would sometimes find myself going up to the first fence in a competition and thinking of something else.

It was then, at a friend's suggestion, that I went to the Leeds Athletic Institute and began to play about wrestling. Straight away I felt the benefit of it. I became more relaxed: show-jumping came easy again. I had got to the stage where it was sweat and toil all day. Wrestling really cleared my mind and got me back on the ball with show-jumping. When I worked on the building site for my father's firm I was alongside working-class lads but as my show-jumping career developed I found myself more and more with the middle and the upper crust. It can't be avoided. My wrestling career has widened the spectrum again and I am the better for it.

Soon I began to take my two lads with me and make it a family outing. I became so keen that I was training three and four times a week and after a while it was mentioned that I might like to have a go in the professional ring. Max Crabtree, a former wrestler, booked me to appear at Newark, after the Newark and Notts Show in 1973.

Being used to performing before crowds, I was not nervous but I did find that I saw the audience in a completely different light. I was more aware of them. A few of the show-jumping boys came to see that first fight and we had a good night. Max fixed up more fights for me and I began to improve.

Because I was a name in show-jumping, I had been forced to have a lot of bouts in the gym so that I could justify my billing, unlike the normal newcomer who can get twelve months in on the circuit before he is expected to be much good. Nevertheless, I had a lot to learn from my opponents. Different fighters have different moves and after they have made them once they don't catch you again. Everything in wrestling has a counter, and it is up to you to find it.

After a while Max started to slip in a few top-liners and it was one of these, Jackie Pallo, who blotted my record. Before I fought Pallo, I went to see him once or twice and Max and I worked on one particular submission hold of his, where he jumps on your back and catches your arms as he goes up. We worked it out that if I folded my arms as he jumped up I could drop him down on to his back and have him.

The fight was at Bradford and Pallo wasn't pleased because he thought I wouldn't be able to hold my own with him. He wanted the fight over sharpish and became more and more exasperated when all the things he came up with didn't work. I got a fall on him in the fourth round and as I turned my back on him he ripped my vest off. That was the start.

In the next round he completely 'lost his rag' and started punching and kneeing. I decided to give him some of it back, collecting a black eye in the process, and it had developed into a bloodbath before the referee stopped the fight and threw us both out of the ring. He had no option, for he could not have cooled tempers down and got us back to wrestling. I should have sat back and left Pallo alone when he had gone too far, as an old pro would have done. Then Pallo would have been thrown out and I would have been awarded the fight. Instead, I turned on the tap and gave him some back.

There was a sequel three weeks later when we met in a bout at Halifax. He was a different man that time, watching himself all the way through, but I beat him two falls to one.

Wrestling is hard work – a full six rounds takes thirty-five minutes – but it can be very enjoyable. I like the fast bouts, hard but with some flair. At other times, you can draw an opponent whose style just does not fit yours. It's all a question of match-making. Wrestling can involve me in travelling between 700 and 1000 miles a week, the Midlands or Wales one night, Scotland the next.

And it does make some of my days busier than ever. An example of a working day at the height of the season: working with a documentary film crew at nine in the morning; off to a show in the afternoon; start a riding demonstration seven p.m., finish at nine-thirty; drive to a wrestling hall for a bout beginning at ten; washed and showered by eleven. After a day like that I don't need a sleeping pill.

The benefits are that I have an extra source of income to fall back on, if and when needed, but far more important that it has taught me to relax again. It keeps me very fit physically, it keeps me supple and it has greatly improved my mental approach to life.

Another activity outside competitive show-jumping which I have recently taken up and found to be very satisfying is giving demonstrations.

Ever since, as a kid at school I used to go on the stage performing with a dog, I have enjoyed entertaining people. This does not mean that I like publicity: there is a distinction between entertaining and publicity-seeking. The entertainment has taken various forms and nowadays my winter calendar is filled with after-dinner speeches, lectures and demonstrations on horseback.

The idea for the demonstrations on horseback came when I was invited to give a lecture at Kevin Francis's indoor school in Sheffield. I thought then that I should mix a little of my after-dinner speeches with some riding instruction: tell them about the showgrounds of the world, riding in general and anything they might want to ask me.

About 250 people turned up for that first appearance.

Nothing followed until I went to Scotland for a wrestling bout and stayed with friends. They asked me if I would give another lecture and demonstration while I was up there and I agreed, partly to help pay my way and partly because I liked the idea. There were some 300 people at that one, near Perth, and my demonstrations built up from then on.

While basically I do the same things with my horse, from elementary groundwork to clearing a five-foot upright, I have found that no two demonstrations are alike. The highlight for me is always when I can get the little kids going. On one occasion a young boy told me of his problem and became engrossed in his explanation. 'My pony won't back. It just goes crazy,' he said. By the time I had finished telling him what to do to get his pony to back he had completely forgotten that he was among several hundred spectators. Then he looked around, realized where he was and shrank back into his seat, but he was happy.

I have found over the years that riding demonstrations tend to be too serious. I try to make them light-hearted at times and to get the crowd going, and I reckon that the way I put over a lesson everyone can grasp the meaning of what I say and do. I have been to demonstrations where only eight or ten people out of a hundred have fully grasped what the instructor has been talking about.

I never prepare for them any more than I do for my after-dinner speeches. Usually I find the organizer when I get to the function and ask him or her: 'Just tell me what you want.' Invariably they are dumbfounded, but I am not being clever. It is just that I find speeches easy to make and, without having to try, I can make people laugh.

I enjoy entertaining people.

16. Banned from the ring

It is surprising how so many people can get misled by the press about how good a year you are having or not having. In 1975, for instance, I didn't have too much success at the Horse of the Year Show or at the big pre-Christmas show at Olympia and because of that, and missing out on television, it seemed to be the general impression that I'd had a lean time throughout the year. Memories can be short.

It is true that the season began more disastrously than any in my show-jumping career. On 4 December 1974 it was announced by the BSJA that Mr Harvey Smith had been in breach of rules 5 (a) (i) and 5 (b) of the Rules and Regulations of the Association when competing at the Empire Pool, Wembley on 14 October. The statement continued: 'The stewards upheld the complaint and directed that Mr Smith be debarred from entering any horse, or jumping, competing or otherwise taking part in any competition at any affiliated show for a period of three months from midnight on 17 December.'

Rule 5 (a) (i) states that no member shall argue at a show with a judge or show official, and 5 (b) that no member shall conduct himself in a manner which in the opinion of the Disciplinary Authority is detrimental to the character and/or prejudicial to the interests of the Association and/or show-jumping.

What was this crime I was supposed to have committed? I was at the Courvoisier Show, which follows the Horse of the Year, and I was riding Speak-Easy. I had not long taken him over from Paul Darragh, who was riding for Trevor Banks and myself, and Speak-Easy was a bit excitable.

He jumped into a combination, and caught the first part

going in. This stopped him dead in his tracks so we went back to start again. When the fence was put back up, the man put up his hand to say it was all clear to go and I started, from fully fifty yards away, coming round to the fence. When I got to within two strides of the fence they still had not sounded the bell, which has to be rung before the round could continue. So I had to stop and they immediately rang it for me to start. My reaction was: 'Where do we go from here?'

I rode across to where the judges were sitting and told them they were judging badly. The complete class was going wrong. Earlier two horses had missed out a fence and yet had been given clear rounds. I did not swear at the judges and limited my remarks to telling them that they were not doing the job as it should be done. Then I went on to finish the round.

At first they announced me as having seven faults – three for a refusal at the second part of the combination, four for having the first part down. That was all right, at least it was better than eight. But after another two horses had been in the ring, they announced that two time penalties had been added to Speak-Easy's score.

Now I knew the three judges in question like the back of my hand. We were all the best of pals before the incident and after it. My criticism of them didn't alter that. But Commander Bill Jefferis the Secretary-General of the BSJA, overheard my remark and instructed the judges to send in a report to the Association. The ban was the outcome.

The decision that my action had been detrimental to the interests of the Association was an interesting one. No member of the press, so far as I know, made any reference to the incident the next day which means that they didn't see or hear anything untoward. And the press are not given to covering up anything concerning me.

I thought then, and still think, that the ban was stupid and unfair. I made one remark and I had my livelihood taken away for three months. Being who I am, I was able to go out wrestling and after-dinner speaking, and so kept a living going. If I hadn't been able to do that I would have had no money coming in for three months.

Basically I don't think the stewards realized just what the sentence could have meant. The Association is not geared to dealing with professional competitors. It is still run with amateur attitudes and that is wrong. It was interesting that, while the ban was still on, one of the BSJA officials rang me and asked what horses I wanted to take to an international show to jump for them after the ban expired. It is a strange organization that can in one breath virtually take away my living and in the next ask me to work for them for nothing.

Maybe it all comes back to Dorian Williams and his suggestion that my influence in show-jumping is undesirable, and that my approach to the sport has taken the fun out of it. Well, all the controversies in which I have been involved have been spontaneous and have come naturally out of competitions. As for fun, show-jumping is not foxhunting. It's a competitive sport. Why should sponsors put up prize money and pay for horses to go to shows throughout the world only to have riders go for a day out rather than try to win? You won't find competitors from other countries going off to a sporting event with that kind of thought in their minds.

In fact, despite the ban with which I started 1975, I finished with three horses in the national Top Ten. Salvador was second to David Broome's Heatwave, Speak-Easy, who doesn't really go indoors and missed Wembley on that account, was sixth and Olympic Star – Foxhunter Champion the year before – was ninth, ahead of Carunna Bay. Salvador also was second to Tauna Dora in the international Top Ten and third to Tauna Dora and Heatwave in the combined international-national list.

Salvador's winnings would have been £2500 higher, too, if a stirrup bar in what was a new saddle had not cut clean through a leather as we were going to the road fence which is number seven in the Wills British Jumping Derby at Hickstead. There wasn't time to get him back into his proper stride and he rolled a pole off. That was his only mistake but it dropped him to fourth place.

Speak-Easy did not have a fence down but met the post-and-rails at the bottom of the bank all wrong and had no option but to refuse. When Salvador won the Derby in 1974 he had only one fence down in the jump-off with Buttevant Boy. He could have had two down and still won in the jump-off against Pele, ridden by Paul Darragh, and Snaffles, who went to pieces with Tony Newberry.

The season had begun well for Salvador when, at his first show, he beat Pennwood Forge Mill in the Radio Rentals Stakes and then Warwick III in the Player's Gold Leaf Stakes at the Devon County Show.

Salvador, Speak-Easy and Olympic Star were all winners at the Bath and West Show and then, again over Reg Whitehead's jumps and courses, they continued in good form at the Royal Cornwall, landing three of the four major classes between them, with Harvest Gold also getting into the act. A slip-up in the second leg of the Professional Championship at Cardiff Castle could not be put right, even though Salvador won the third leg, and so I tied with David for second place behind Stephen Hadley who rode sensibly on Carunna Bay after pipping Salvador on time in the first leg.

At Dublin where Salvador had jumped a double clear in the Aga Khan Cup the year before, he was in the winning team again and there was no need for David to jump Heat-wave in the second round, Forge Mill having gone clear and Tauna Dora having had four faults, like Salvador.

Other journeys abroad helped to top up Salvador's winnings without bringing in enough to get him into the top spot in the international Top Ten.

17. Then and now

I have seen enormous changes in show-jumping since I first started competing in major competitions over twenty years ago. Then it was very much a minority interest whereas now it is a fast-growing and enormously spectator-orientated sport involving large sums of money.

It is, of course, becoming harder than ever to win a major show-jumping competition because the standard has risen throughout the world. No mediocre horse can get away with anything now. The highest fence in the Olympic Games of 1948 was 4 feet 6 inches. Now they get to 5 feet 6 inches or 5 feet 8 inches, and one wall in the last Olympics was 6 feet.

If we look back at the early 1960s there were leading horses of the calibre of Sunsalve and Wildfire, both ridden by David Broome, and O'Malley. Ted Williams always had four or five really good horses, and there were also Sue Cohen – I remember she went into the White City once and won five or six classes off the reel, no mean achievement – George Hobbs, Peter Robeson and Alan Oliver. Anneli Drummond-Hay was just starting and Ann Townsend soon came to the fore. All were in the top rank but basically there was only a handful to contend with. Now there are far more good riders and good horses although the good young ones tend to come and go. We have lost Ted but David, Peter and myself are still here, as is Paddy McMahon. Even if none of the three of us is eligible for the Olympic Games.

In the early 1960s horses did not travel abroad so much and we used to lay off the horses in the winter, so that they would come back fresh in the spring. Now the season goes on virtually all year and just as English riders go more and more to the Continent, so the Continentals – especially the Germans – have become frequent visitors here.

The people who run the sport have very often failed to move with the times. Apart from generally applying an amateurish approach to what is now a major sport, it sometimes seems that show-jumping has become popular in spite of, rather than because of, their efforts. Show-jumping is entertainment and should be run as such.

Basically, a show-jumping programme at a show where the public have paid to get in should consist of a 13.2 hands or 14.2 hands class for the top junior ponies, a top-grade novice class, an Open for the seniors and, perhaps, a Grades B and C just to round off the day. The lesser competitions have no entertainment value and the adults and children who have the horses and ponies which compete in them should have their fun and enjoyment at special minor shows.

Ponies can be good entertainment. Occasionally you get a little girl in plaits going over 5 feet with a 13.2 hands pony and that is giving the public value for money. And yet the juniors are badly done by when it comes to prize money. I have known them jump for £7 in a televised Hickstead competition, which should not be allowed. There should never be prizes of under £15 for a junior class.

And even if the programmes were organized as I believe they should be, the show needs speeding up. No competition should last more than about an hour and a quarter and, if fifty or sixty horses could go in that time, that would be top entertainment. This would mean an end to the modern idea of courses half a mile long. They wear out the horses and the public. Shorter courses and a restricted time in the ring are what is required. At the moment people can have a picnic between rounds at some shows.

I have been involved in the pony-jumping scene because both of my lads, Robert and Stephen, are keen riders. In their early show-jumping days the boys frequently rode against each other and they were keen rivals. When they finished equal first at one particular show they refused to divide and had a stand-up fight.

Not that it had all been plain sailing with either of them. Irene and I started them riding when they were eight and seven and it can be a hard slog with boys of that age. Girls take to horses and ponies and will work with them all day long. Lads will work to a certain degree and then want to be off playing football or cricket, or climbing trees. Anyway, we were double keen to get them going and I made a mistake by buying ponies which were just a bit big for them. That didn't help and after a time I agreed with Irene's suggestion that we should leave them alone.

So we bought electric trains and bikes and every time they came to us and asked to go out riding with us we would tell them to go and play with their toys. This had been going on for a while when I came across a donkey who was just the sort I was looking for. It never bucked or kicked, it walked quietly and it would canter on. The lads fell in line with it and were ready when a pal of mine offered to lend me a very quiet pony. They didn't have to be persuaded to go riding from then on.

At first, riding came more easily to Stephen, the younger of the two, than it did to Robert but lads mature quickly in their teens and it is Robert who has developed the more quickly in show-jumping. He will work and listen. I don't drill him and try instead to leave him alone to do his own thing. If he has any problems, then he comes to me. I will check on him maybe twice or three times a week and see him at no more than eight shows a year. He is educating himself and that is far better than having someone bellowing at him.

If I do see him make a mistake, then I will tell him and he will just sit back and take it in. A lot of kids are inclined to get off and blame the pony when things go wrong. On the very odd occasion that Robert has done that, I have proved to him immediately that it wasn't the pony's fault, so that he realizes now that 95 per cent of mistakes made in the ring are made by the jockey.

Inevitably, Robert's schooling has suffered in some ways through his active interest in show-jumping but I believe that going through life and meeting people is the finest education of all. I'm not decrying the local kids who come to the farm to play with Robert and Stephen, but they are nowhere near as advanced as my lads. While both my lads may be losing education in the book fashion they are gaining a great deal more practical experience of life than they could in the classroom. Practice is better than theory any time.

Not long ago, Robert told me that he would never smoke or drink. He has been around the shows and he has been able to come to such a decision perhaps five years or more before he might have done with a more secluded upbringing.

Behind both lads is the security of my farm, with its beef cattle and sheep. If they don't want to go show-jumping they do not need to do so. Yet Robert knows the feeling of going in front of 8000 people at Wembley and that gives a better boost than any doctor can administer. He says he wants to ride horses for a living and I believe he will. Stephen is too young to make up his mind yet but certainly I would be pleased if he followed suit. It would be satisfying if one day they could jump with me for Britain in a Nations Cup team.

What with working with the boys, competing as hard as ever, giving lectures and demonstrations, farming, and wrestling, life now is busier than it has ever been. Yet I find time to keep my experienced horses going and bring on youngsters. The indoor school, which we put up at Craiglands Farm in 1968, has helped a lot here.

Indoor jumping has grown rapidly in the last decade and now horses are more used to jumping under artificial light than they are out of doors. Other commitments permitting, I like to work my horses in the morning, try to concentrate on farming in the afternoon and then do quite a bit of work again with the horses at night. It can be peaceful at night and I can work out my problems nice and quietly with my horses for two or three hours at a stretch without breaking off to answer the telephone or see to a caller.

Usually at night I get several horses out and school them, trying out different things and all the time getting moulded into the horses. In the old days I used to have fewer horses and spent more time with them. Without the indoor school I had to ride them for a long time to get them concentrating and listening. In the indoor school they can't look out and see anything else to take their minds off their work so they do concentrate more quickly, but there are dangers. Horses can get stale, and if they have had too much work inside they can be raving lunatics when they get into the open air. Indoor and outdoor training must be balanced.

The whole purpose of the training, wherever it takes place, is to get the horses to enjoy what they are doing while at the same time knowing that I am in command. When they go into the ring they must know at the backs of their minds that I am in charge and yet be relaxed. I have always seen the training of my horses as just as important a part of my job as what happens in the show-jumping arena.

To me show-jumping has always been far more than winning money. I supose the great majority of sportsmen, especially in sports where it is one man against the rest, see their part in it as a challenge. There has never been anything I like better than to buy a horse, improve it and then go out and beat all the others. This is particularly true in the case of a misfit with whom other riders have been unable to get on. Among my later horses, Salvador falls into that category; War Paint was one of my early ones.

Even before I made the first move in British show-jumping towards becoming a professional it was said repeatedly of me that I was in the game only for money. Yet if the prize money had been nowhere near the level it was I would still have been in the job. The rewards anyway were not always staggeringly high in the 1960s and, although they have improved, they could still be higher nowadays. When O'Malley equalled the North American high-jump record with a leap of 7 feet 3 inches on the 1967 tour, all we received was a ribbon.

I have always believed that people who get buckled down to the job of winning should be rewarded for it, not hammered, and it is this that has often led to clashes with authority during my career. My battles tend to be fought alone as many people involved in show-jumping are happy to have their battles fought for them. I remember what an old fellow told me when I was just starting out: 'The wind always blows strongest on the tallest tree', and I like to think that I prove the saying.

My main driving force has always been the will to win. Choose whatever I do, I have to win. If I was racing one of my lads down the road I could not let him beat me. And if I am beaten fair and square, I analyse what went wrong and make damned sure that I am not beaten for the same reason again.

That goes for my show-jumping, my wrestling, everything I do. There would be no point in going on if the will to win wasn't there.

Glossary

Backing: The stage of breaking in a young horse when the rider first gets on its back.

BSJA: British Show Jumping Association.

Cavaletti: A single pole suported by cross-bars, about a foot from the ground. Used for schooling horses.

Chef d'équipe: Team captain, usually non-competing.

Collecting ring: The ring outside the arena in which riders warm their horses up.

FEI: Fédération Equestre Internationale, the international ruling body for equestrian sports.

Foxhunter competition: A competition for novice horses.

Gamblers competition: An event in which competitors can jump fences in any order from any direction. Each fence cleared is worth a certain number of points, depending on how difficult they are, and competitors have to gain as high a score as possible within a time limit.

Grades A, B, and C: Grades of show-jumping competitions, the qualifications for which are based on money which has been won by horses, e.g. only horses who have won more than £400 can compete in Grade A events.

Hand: A measure of height for horses, equal to four inches.

Have-a-gamble: Same as Gamblers competition.

Hobday: An operation on a horse's windpipe.

Martingale: a piece of saddlery, of which there are several types, designed to prevent a horse throwing its head about.

Mouthing: The process of getting a young horse used to a bit and bridle.

Napping: A horse that ducks out and tries to avoid working is said to nap.

Nations Cup: International team events.

Navicular: An incurable bone disease which can affect horses' legs.

President's Cup: Award for the country which has won the most points in Nations Cups throughout the season.

Puissance: Show-jumping's high-jump competition. At the end of the puissance, horses remaining in the competition usually have to jump two jumps, a big spread and the wall.

Rapping: Illegal method of schooling show-jumpers.

Scopey: A horse with 'scope', often described as 'scopey', is one that is cable of jumping big, wide spreads.

Snaffle: a type of bit.

Index

Compiled by Susan Kennedy